Caving

Caving

Peter Swart

First published in 2002 by
New Holland Publishers Ltd
London • Cape Town • Sydney • Auckland
www.newhollandpublishers.com

US edition published by Stackpole Books

All inquiries should be addressed to
Stackpole Books
5067 Ritter Road
Mechanicsburg PA 17055

2 4 6 8 10 9 7 5 3 1

First Edition

ISBN 0-8117-2052-7

Publisher: Mariëlle Renssen
Managing Editors: Claudia dos Santos, Simon Pooley
Managing Art Editor: Richard MacArthur
Commissioning Editor: Karyn Richards
Editor: Lauren Copley
Designer: Christelle Marais
Illustrator: David Vickers
Picture researcher: Karla Kik
Production: Myrna Collins
Consultant: Graham Price (UK)

Reproduction by Hirt & Carter (Cape) Pty Ltd
Printed and bound in Singapore by Craft Print (Pte) Ltd

Library of Congress Cataloging-in-Publication Data

Swart, P.K. (Peter K.)
Caving / Peter Swart.
p. cm.
ISBN 0-8117-2052-7 (alk. paper)
1. Caving I. Title.

GV200.62 .S93 2002
796.52'5—dc21   2002022597

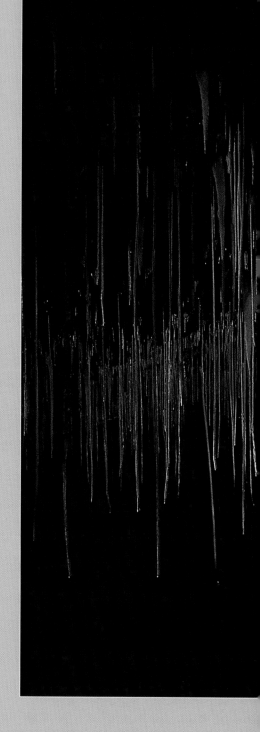

Disclaimer

This handbook should not be used as a substitute for lessons from a certified professional caving instructor. Nothing in this book should be read as advice to undertake dangerous maneuvers or explore underground environments without proper guidance and training. Although the author and publishers

have made every effort to ensure that the information contained in this book was accurate at the time of going to press, they accept no responsibility for any accident, loss or inconvenience that is sustained by any person using this book or the advice given in it.

Author's acknowledgments

I would like to thank Anthony Hitchcock for introducing me to cave surveying and being my constant caving companion for the past 20 years, Dr Steve Craven for his encouragement over the years, and Stephan Moser and Greg Waller for their valued technical input and assistance. My fellow cavers for the many enjoyable caving trips, Pat Hitchcock for all the post-caving coffee, and Nadine for her support with this book. Last but not least, to my mother, Mavis: I thank you for all the caving overalls you have washed over the years — this book is dedicated to you.

Contents

Introduction

Exploring hidden territory

I am prepared to admit that this man-serpent game, with its prospect of having to lie, sometimes for hours, on nasty cold rock, in mud or icy water, rubbing the skin off elbows, knees, and all parts of the body, is not everyone's idea of enjoyment. Can people really be thrilled by activities so repellent, dangerous, unhealthy, and possibly useless? Is there not beauty and variety enough under the vault of heaven, that a man must go and grope his way blindly at enormous labor, plunging down deliberately into the darkness of the nether regions and all the pitfalls it contains?

NORBERT CASTERET (1897—1987)

this is what French explorer and adventurer Norbert Casteret, one of the world's first professional speleologists, had to say about caving. His quote summarizes what caving is all about both physically and in spirit. It mentions some of the physical hardships that form part of caving — the cold rocks, copious amounts of mud and icy water. It also touches on the potential dangers, an aspect with which he was very familiar.

During Casteret's caving career, he broke almost every modern safety rule. This included diving alone through flooded passages to explore remote parts of caves, with no more than a few damp candles to light the way. After highlighting just how unpleasant caving can be, Casteret asks the question that most cavers ask themselves at some stage or another: 'Is there not beauty enough under the vault of heaven?' In other words, why go caving at all?

Quest for curiosity

As caving covers such a wide range of activities on so many different levels, finding out why people venture underground has as many pitfalls as cavers may encounter on their subterranean journeys. The common thread, however tenuous, is curiosity. This curiosity takes many forms. For some it is a quest to find out more about themselves and explore their personal limits. They are continually searching for deeper tunnels to descend or narrower passages to negotiate, pitting themselves mentally or physically against whatever obstacles are put in their way. They

push themselves a little further each time in their quest to determine the inner limit. For others, it is an inquisitiveness born out of a quest for knowledge.

This was what started Casteret on his underground career. Initially, his interest in prehistory led him in search of the clues that early man had left in caves, until the caves themselves became more important to him than their contents. This is not an unusual introduction into the sport. Whether the caver starts out as a biologist interested in cave animals, or a chemist interested in the process of cave formation, the result is often the same. Their fields of interest lead them into a cave, and before they know it caving becomes as important as the inquisitiveness that brought them there in the first place.

Whatever it is that motivates the very first trip, curiosity about the caves themselves soon becomes an important reason for this risky pursuit. Cavers are always wondering what lies around the next corner, or on the other side of the boulder and even what lies beneath their feet.

Like any other explorer, every caver dreams of a major breakthrough — discovering a new and unknown cave or a new passage. Cavers constantly question, probe and explore the limits to find a clue that may lead them to discovery.

opposite WATER POURS INTO THIS PARTIALLY FLOODED CAVE PASSAGE IN PUERTO RICO. DRIPSTONE FORMATIONS CANNOT FORM IN SUCH STRONG FLOWS, THEY REQUIRE A MUCH SLOWER, STEADIER DRIP.

THIS CAVE IN BORNEO DISPLAYS THE CHARACTERISTIC ROUNDED CROSS SECTION OF A PHREATIC PASSAGE. IT WAS FORMED AT A TIME WHEN THE GROUNDWATER TABLE WAS MUCH HIGHER, FLOODING THE PASSAGE AND ALLOWING THE LIMESTONE TO DISSOLVE EVENLY.

Why the darkness beckons

Curiosity may be the common thread running through the many reasons for caving, but it is not a reason in itself to venture underground. For many, the sheer adventure and excitement of seeking out obstacles and the satisfaction of overcoming them are motivation enough to consider caving as a leisure activity.

But is caving a sport? There are elements of caving that are definitely sporting. The rush of adrenaline as you step off the lip of a chasm and commit your life to a thin nylon rope on your descent into darkness has to be experienced first-hand to be appreciated. The smaller sections of caves are no less exciting. Imagine squeezing through a narrow vertical crack with nothing but darkness ahead, a solid rock wall jammed hard against your back and the opposite wall hemming you in from the front. When your heartbeat pounds so loudly in your ears that you are convinced someone is hammering on the rock that surrounds you — this, too, can be exciting. Not surprisingly, many cavers believe the excitement generated by the sporting side of caving is the only reason to cave.

Whenever you venture underground, you find yourself surrounded by an environment that is in stark contrast to anything you will have seen above ground. Yet, even though the subterranean environment is very different, certain parallels do exist.

In essence, if a particular 'above-ground activity', such as photography for example, appeals to you, you are likely to find this interest stimulated underground, with the added challenge that you will have to learn how to cope with completely different surroundings and circumstances — and the restrictions they impose. Caving can thus become a vehicle to explore and discover exciting new aspects of favorite pastimes, in this case underground photography.

Although many people begin caving for the adventure, once they have mastered the techniques, the adventure itself is often no longer enough to sustain their interest, so many turn to one of the more specialized areas of caving (and some give up).

For some avid photographers, when the beauty and variety of nature above ground is not enough, they are attracted by the daunting prospect of journeying into the depths of the earth in order to capture breathtaking visual images under less than ideal conditions. For them, there is no better place than the dark realms of a cave to capture geological curiosities, improbable dripstone formations and beautiful, seemingly otherworldly vistas.

Those who enjoy the thrill of exploration, for example, will make a relatively logical progression to pacing out and measuring what they have found. In the case of caves this involves drawing detailed maps. In technical terms, this is known as cave surveying (see pages 74–78) and the maps that are produced are called surveys. Nowadays, well-organized teams put enormous amounts of effort into measuring every opening and little passage in a cave system to produce impressively detailed maps.

One of the most specialized forms of caving is cave diving, which has been described as the most risky outdoor pursuit in the world. Cave divers are a special breed. They combine the skills of maneuvering safely underwater with exploring underground waterways. The dangers associated with surviving underwater in artificial conditions are multiplied during a cave dive. In addition, divers may need to spend hours or even days underground just to reach the start of their dive.

All of the above shows that caving is a very diverse activity. It provides an adventure playground for some and a career for others. Where will you fit in?

CAVE DIVING IS HIGHLY SPECIALIZED AND DANGEROUS. THIS WARNING SIGN IN AN UNDERWATER CAVE ON THE YUCATÁN PENINSULA CAUTIONS INEXPERIENCED DIVERS NOT TO PROCEED.

Cave Formation

before you venture underground, it is useful to learn a little about caves, how they are formed and what you may expect to find.

Even though one dominant forming process may have been — or may still be — at work in a cave, more often a combination of factors is involved. Some of the major processes are covered in these pages.

Solution caves

To a traditional caver from Kentucky the world of geology is fairly simple: only two types of rock exist, limestone and everything else. This is because most of the world's big caves are formed of limestone or other carbonate-based rock such as predominates in this part of the US. Since limestone caves form when parent rock is dissolved, they are known as Solution Caves.

Limestone is a sedimentary rock chiefly made up of calcium carbonate. The sediments from which the rock is formed

were deposited in lakes and on ocean floors countless years ago. Over time, heat and pressure in the earth's crust turned these layers (strata) into hard limestone. In some cases, the original sediment layers (beds) stayed separate during the hardening process.

While the hardening process was taking place, the part of the earth's crust on which the sediments were positioned experienced subtle movement. This caused vertical tension fractures to appear in the young rock, much like a facial mask would crack if the wearer smiled. These cracks are known as joints. The result was a block of rock crisscrossed with fissures and cracks in all directions.

Although later geological processes and violent upheaval may have changed the orientation of horizontal and vertical planes, let us stay with a simple model for the moment, where beds are horizontal and joints vertical. An important feature of limestone is that it readily dissolves, even in a very weak acid solution. Horizontal beds of soluble limestone rock interspersed with vertical joints are the ideal building block for the creation of caves — and the process begins from above.

When raindrops fall through the air on their journey from the cloud formation to earth, they combine with the carbon dioxide present in the atmosphere to form carbonic acid. This weak solution is just what is required to dissolve limestone.

The vertical cracks that were formed so many thousands of years ago make ideal points of entry for the rain. Carbonic-acid-laced rain

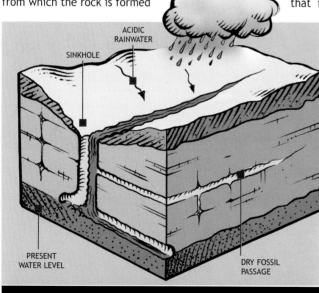

ACIDIC RAINWATER

SINKHOLE

PRESENT WATER LEVEL

DRY FOSSIL PASSAGE

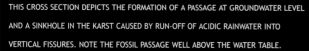

THIS CROSS SECTION DEPICTS THE FORMATION OF A PASSAGE AT GROUNDWATER LEVEL AND A SINKHOLE IN THE KARST CAUSED BY RUN-OFF OF ACIDIC RAINWATER INTO VERTICAL FISSURES. NOTE THE FOSSIL PASSAGE WELL ABOVE THE WATER TABLE.

opposite SPECTACULAR DRIP- AND FLOWSTONE FORMATIONS SURROUND A SHALLOW UNDERGROUND POOL IN A NEW MEXICO CAVE CREATING AN ENCHANTED SUBTERRANEAN WONDERLAND MADE OF SPARKLING CRYSTALS.

trickles into the rock mass and goes to work. When the rainwater passes through an acidic layer of soil, it absorbs the acids, becoming stronger. If this acidic water falls on limestone, it finds its way deeper into the rock via the joints and openings between the different beds. On its way through, the acidic solution gradually dissolves the limestone and thus widens any crack or crevice in its path. Over millions of years, small cracks enlarged into the cave passages that modern cavers explore so eagerly today.

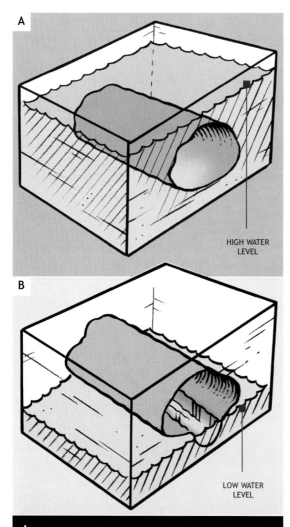

A

HIGH WATER LEVEL

B

LOW WATER LEVEL

A PHREATIC PASSAGES FORM WHEN THE WATER TABLE LIES ABOVE THE PASSAGE ROOF, THEREBY COMPLETELY FILLING IT AND CAUSING THE LIMESTONE-SATURATED WATER TO ESCAPE VERY SLOWLY.

B A KEYHOLE PASSAGE RESULTS WHEN THE WATER TABLE DROPS. THE FLOW SPEEDS UP AND DISSOLUTION OCCURS AT A FASTER RATE.

Types of cave passages

Two main types of cave passages form under the conditions described above. The first, known as phreatic passage, is formed when the entire passage is below the level of the water table and the movement of acidic groundwater through the passage is relatively slow. The second occurs where groundwater flows relatively fast above the water table and there is usually an airspace between the water surface and the cave ceiling. These are called vadose passages.

In the first case, where passages are fully submerged and water movement is slow, the limestone that is dissolved from the passage walls quickly saturates the water. The dissolution process cannot continue until fresh, unsaturated water flows into the system. Passages formed under these conditions tend to have very rounded cross sections. In vadose passages water moves quickly and so, as soon as the limestone is dissolved, the water is replaced by unsaturated water. This kind of flow creates canyon-like passages that are narrow and deep.

Cave passage formation often involves a combination of the phreatic and vadose processes. A typical case occurs when a phreatic passage originally forms below the surface of the water table: it will have a typically rounded cross section. As the water table drops, groundwater flow through the cave system speeds up and changes to a vadose-type of development, which results in keyhole-shaped passages. In caves where the groundwater table has dropped so low that no water is present at all, you may find what is sometimes labelled fossil passages, i.e. dry passages. This term indicates that no further enlargement is evident or in progress.

Although only subterranean processes have been described here, very similar forces are at work shaping the landscape on the surface. In early geological times, fissures exposed by tectonic action on the surface were widened and the resulting network of cracks that led to the maze of passages below ground formed a landscape characteristic of limestone regions. Known as karst, it is named after the limestone Karst plateau near Trieste.

Features of karst

One of the typical features of a karst landscape are sinkholes. These occur where underground chambers form close to the surface. When the roof of this chamber collapses, the result is a depression in the ground. Sinkholes vary in depth and width from a few meters or feet to enormous pits. The collapses are known as dolines and, in many cases, they provide entrance to extensive cave systems below.

The telltale signs of karst landscapes are as follows:

■ Rivers that seem to sink or disappear into the ground.

■ Rivers that seem to spring or appear from the ground.

■ Rivers that do not follow the surface topography naturally, but often pass underneath mountain ranges.

■ Underground caves.

■ Pavement surfaces (exposed flat surface rock areas that exhibit solutional features).

■ Potholes or collapses.

■ Rock outcrops whose surfaces display the incisions of water-worn channels.

Although these features are most commonly associated with limestone or other carbonate-based rocks, some also occur in non-carbonate rocks such as sandstone. Since sandstone is not as soluble as limestone, most caves formed in this rock are caused by erosion and they usually do not amount to more than alcoves. Where true solution caves have formed in sandstone, they tend to be very small and seldom exceed a few hundred meters or feet in length, although exceptional cases that measure several kilometers do exist.

A landform that has the look of a karst region but was not formed by dissolution is known as pseudokarst.

THIS IMPRESSIVE AERIAL PICTURE OF THE KARST LANDSCAPE AROUND THE LLANGATOCK AND LLANGYNIDR MOUNTAINS IN SOUTHERN WALES DISPLAYS A VAST AMOUNT OF COLLAPSED SINKHOLES THAT CAN INDICATE AN AREA OF MAJOR CAVE DEVELOPMENT.

THE POWERFUL ABRASIVE EFFECT THAT ROCKS SUSPENDED IN FAST-MOVING WATER CAN HAVE IS CLEARLY SEEN IN THIS DRAMATIC EXAMPLE OF AN EROSION CAVE, WHICH FORMED IN GRANITE. NOTICE THE ROUND, EVENLY SHAPED CAVITIES AND WALLS.

Erosion caves

Both solution and erosion caves are formed when the original bedrock is removed, leaving cavities. The difference between the two types of cave formation is how it is removed. In a solution cave chemical reaction dissolves the rock; in an erosion cave the cause is a mechanical process. The main prerequisites for the formation of an erosion cave are a pre-existing cavity in the rock, a fluid of some kind (usually water) which transports a scourer, and a scouring agent that whittles the rock away.

The process is very simple. Water carrying abrasive particles in suspension flows through the cavity. As it does so, the particles begin to wear away the walls and enlarge the cavity. Particles do not have to be small. Large boulders can also be agents of erosion. An example of this is a rock made of a hard material that becomes trapped in a depression in a stream bed made of a softer material. If the stream is powerful enough it will move the rock around within this depression, creating a grinding action. Any trapped sand particles act as 'grinding paste' and together the two will wear away the softer stream bed to create a pothole.

Erosion is usually a secondary cave-forming process — a cavity or depression already has to exist. This means that erosion frequently occurs in caves that were initially formed by solution, but it is not always the case. As the earth's crust moves, new cracks and faults are created continually in all types of rock. When a strong stream finds such a newly formed entrance in any kind of rock, and if the crack is large enough, the erosion process can begin. The resulting passages are usually a combination of deep cylindrical potholes and canyon-like passages.

Washout caves

Washout caves are very similar to erosion caves in that here, too, material is carried out by water. The difference between the two processes is that erosion wears away a solid mass of rock, while a washout is formed by the removal of loose material that does not have to be worn down. This type of cave occurs where the surrounding parent rock is not solid, but comprises either gravel or conglomerate (a sedimentary rock consisting of round stone fragments embedded in a finer agent). Small particles of sand between larger pebbles are washed away until a sufficient hole is created and a pebble is loosened. When enough small material has been removed the pebbles will have nothing left to support them and will, in turn, be washed out of the newly formed pipe. This process eventually leads to the development of a cave.

Ice caves

Not all caves occur in rock. Although not everyone agrees that cavities and shafts that have formed in ice can be termed real caves, they can provide some very exciting caving.

Glaciers are rivers of ice that grind slowly down valleys in much the same way water does. During warm periods, meltwater (with a temperature slightly warmer than the surrounding ice) finds its way into various cracks and crevices and begins to enlarge them until they become cave passages.

Glaciers, however, are not the only places where ice caves can form. In the colder regions of the world — wherever large, brittle plates of ice form, such as Greenland and Antarctica — any earth movements, and even changes in gravity or shifts in temperature will cause the mantle of ice to crack. The resulting fissures sometimes reach hundreds of meters deep into the plate.

WITH STRATEGICALLY PLACED ROPES SECURELY ANCHORED INTO THE SURROUNDING ICE WALLS TO ENSURE HIS SAFE DESCENT, A CAVER GETS READY TO ABSEIL DOWN INTO A STEEP CAVE SHAFT IN THE FOX GLACIER, NEW ZEALAND.

Erosion caves are found along the coasts of countries around the world. This is due to the fact that two key factors required for their formation occur along coastlines: there is no shortage of moving water and abrasive sand. Whether the caves form or not depends on the geology of the coast.

In land-based erosion cave water has to flow along and down a crack in order to wear away the sides and enlarge it. At the sea-side the powerful action of the waves beating against the coast repeatedly forces seawater into cracks in the rocks, sucking it out again as the wave retreats. This washing back and forth of the sea replaces the flowing action of a stream in an inland cave.

Suspended in the water, abrasive agents like shells and particles of sand are repeatedly washed up against the rocks. This action exploits any fault or weakness it finds and will, in time, scour deeper and deeper to produce a sea cave. Cracks and faults in coastal rock that lie perpendicular (at right angles) to the direction of the waves are, of course, the easiest targets. They are, however, not the only cause.

Another very common type of sea cave occurs in sedimentary rock, which consists of different strata, where the sedimentary bed is made up of a softer material than the surrounding layers. In this scenario, abrasive wave action removes the softer bedding plane much faster than it can carve into the harder rock, thus creating a cave passage. These caves tend to be short and straight, usually no more than a few hundred meters long.

Since many sea caves formed at a time when the sea level was either higher or much lower than it is today, a great number are now submerged or occur inland of the present-day coast.

TWO SEA CAVES IN THE DEEPLY INCISED COAST OF LUNDY ISLAND, NEAR THE BRISTOL CHANNEL ON THE SOUTHWEST COAST OF ENGLAND. THE COASTAL CLIFF HAS BEEN ERODED BY CENTURIES OF RHYTHMICALLY POUNDING WAVE ACTION.

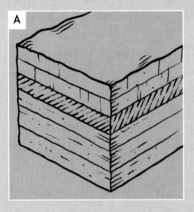

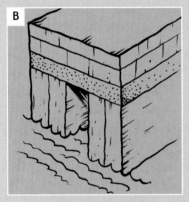

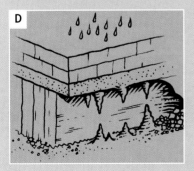

Sea cave formation

Many of the sea caves along the coast of Southern Africa have formed between thick beds of hard quartzite, but some are also decorated by calcite formations. This series of diagrams first shows the formation of the parent rock structure and then the subsequent cave-forming process.

A In the very distant past, layers of sediment settled at the bottom of a lake or calm inland sea. In this example, one layer consisted of finer-grained sediment.

Over millions of years, changes in the earth's crust exerted immense heat and pressure on the beds. This changed them from coarse-grained sandstone into hard quartzite. During this time, the finer-grained material changed into shale (soft, compressed rock layers of fine-grained mud or clay).

B The same immense forces that began to crush and compress the sedimentary beds in the Mesozoic era (from 225 million to around 65 million years ago) also tilted them until they had been pushed into a near vertical position. After this, yet more layers of fine sediment were deposited. In more recent geological history, a layer of wind-borne calcareous (chalky) sea sand was blown over the top of the cliffs.

C When changing sea levels began to expose the tilted beds to the sea, wave action began to erode the bed of soft shale, leaving behind a tall, narrow, straight cave wedged between quartzite beds. (In caves like this, traces of the shale band can often still be seen on the ceiling.)

Subsequent changes in sea level washed sand and boulders into the cave, partially filling it at times, then scouring it again.

Changes in sea conditions occurring in the Tertiary period (around 70 million years ago) resulted in much of the former deposit being washed out to sea. As the sea receded it exposed remnants of layered fill at the back of the cave: the distinct layers of previous deposits.

D Sea levels then remained low for long enough to allow calcite decorations to form. Even though the cave had formed in quartzite, acidic rainwater percolating through the layers of calcareous sea sand above was able to accumulate enough calcium carbonate to begin the formation of stalagmites and stalactites.

Lava tubes

The cave formations described so far began with a piece of rock being worn away either by chemical or mechanical erosion, or sometimes both, leaving a cave surrounded by the remaining host rock. Lava tubes are different because the surrounding rock is deposited while the cave is being formed.

Lava tubes are exactly what the name implies — passages formed in lava. When molten lava flows from a volcano over open ground, its top layer is exposed to the atmosphere and cools down. As it cools it solidifies, forming a hard crust over the top and sides of the flow, which acts as an insulator and slows down the release of heat into the atmosphere. The bottom of the flow rests on the ground, also acting as an insulator. The molten flow is thus confined within a thermally insulated pipe, which keeps it warm and fluid.

Provided that the lower end of the pipe is not blocked, the lava will continue to flow through the tube even after the source of the flow is cut off from the volcano. The pipe will slowly drain itself of lava, leaving behind the crust that kept it insulated.

The result is a tube created entirely of solidified lava that can sometimes be several kilometers or miles long. This type of cave commonly occurs in places such as Hawaii and the Canary Islands where there are many active and dormant volcanoes.

Movement caves

Movement caves are neither hollowed out like erosion caves nor built up like lava caves. They occur when powerful tectonic movements open fissures in the upper layer of the earth's mantle. The caves literally form where the earth is being pulled apart and so caves

THIS LARGE LAVA TUBE IN CALIFORNIA, FORMED DURING A VIOLENT VOLCANIC ERUPTION LONG AGO, GIVES AN INDICATION OF THE ENORMOUS AMOUNTS OF LAVA THAT FLOWED DOWN THE SLOPES. TODAY IT MAKES A PERFECT DESTINATION FOR CAVERS.

Another type of 'built cave'

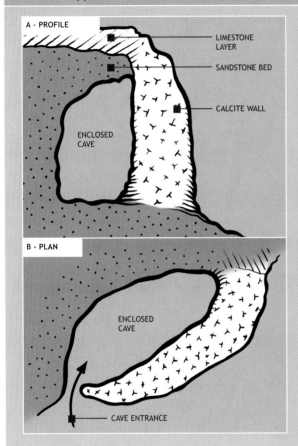

A - PROFILE

LIMESTONE LAYER

SANDSTONE BED

CALCITE WALL

ENCLOSED CAVE

B - PLAN

ENCLOSED CAVE

CAVE ENTRANCE

Lava tubes are not the only examples of 'built' caves. In a limestone cave, water dissolves the limestone and carries it away. Some of the dissolved matter is redeposited as calcium carbonate inside the cave, where it begins to form decorations. On occasion, however, the dissolved rock is carried away and deposited outside the cave. This type of deposit is called travertine.

This illustration of a travertine formation (left), is depicted in (A) side and (B) top elevation. The cave here was created in a typical two-step process. First a river cut a winding gorge through a region of fine-grained sandstone beds. At each turn, the swirling river undercut sections of the rocky riverbank, leaving large overhangs. In time, these would either have collapsed or remained as overhangs with a thin overlaying deposit of limestone. Rainwater began to dissolve this layer, but redeposited it as it flowed over the cliff edge.

Over time, the formations grew large enough to join together from above and below, forming a wall over the entrance to the overhang and thus creating a completely enclosed cave.

formed in this way will often display matching features on opposite walls. If one wall has a rock protruding from it, an examination of the opposite wall will reveal a hole similar in size (left when the fissure opened and the rock was pulled away).

Yet another type of cave that is created by movement, albeit a completely different type, is the talus cave. Talus is nothing more than the pile of boulders that usually collects at the bottom of mountain slopes. As a mountain slope erodes, boulders break away and roll down to collect in a heap at the bottom. If enough large boulders break away and tumble down to form a sufficiently large heap, the gaps between them become big enough to be considered a cave. Talus caves can provide some extremely challenging caving.

VERTICAL CRACKS AS DEEP AS CANYONS SCORE THE LIMESTONE LAYER OF THIS REGION PRODUCING WHAT IS TERMED A KARST LANDSCAPE. BELOW THE GROUND WILL BE SIMILAR GORGES AND SUBTERRANEAN STREAMS.

Cave decorations

A STRAW FORMATIONS.
B FLOWSTONE COLUMNS AND STALACTITES.
C FLOWSTONE WITH NEW STALACTITE.

One of the unbeatable rewards of underground exploration is the discovery of cave decorations varying from tiny crystals to massive columns. After mud, the most common type of cave deposit is calcite, which is the ingredient that creates some of the most awesome underground scenery imaginable. Calcite results when the chemical process that forms caves is reversed. Instead of limestone dissolving in water, it precipitates out and is deposited to form decorations.

Decorations that form from the top down begin when calcium carbonate-laden water seeps through cracks and crevices in the cave roof and drops to the ground or runs down a wall. As soon as this water comes into contact with the dry cave air it begins to evaporate, which lowers the water's capacity to hold the dissolved calcium carbonate in solution. What is left behind becomes a cave decoration.

■ When a deposit is made around the edge of a hanging water drop, a rim forms around it. Subsequent deposits lead to the formation of a delicate tube-like decoration called **straw**. Although these can on occasion reach 3m (10ft) in length, they seldom measure more than 6–9mm ($\frac{1}{4}$–$\frac{1}{3}$in) in diameter. If the straw becomes blocked by crystal formations or debris, side growths may appear at the point where water leaks from the hollow center.

■ If water runs over the outside of a formation rather than down a tube in the middle, an icicle-shaped **stalactite** is formed. Stalactites can reach impressive diameters and lengths.

■ **Flowstone**, which comprises curtains and ridges of calcite, forms when water trickles down cave walls instead of dripping from the ceiling. The water does not run in streams but coats the rock in a thin film, depositing calcite in a formation that re-sembles a large frozen waterfall.

■ Some formations grow from the bottom up. When a drop falls from the bottom of a straw or stalactite, it loses more of its water content on its way down, leaving a deposit of calcite where it lands. Sometimes small calcite-filled holes are all that results, but more often **stalagmites** form. Some of these are known to have reached a truly impressive 50m (160ft) in diameter.

■ **Helictites** are decorations that seem to defy gravity. They can form in any direction. These very attractive shapes are caused in calcite deposits where crystal formation takes place at a faster rate than gravity. This leads to adventurously crinkled decorations with spectacular twists.

■ **Rimstone pools** grow from the bottom up, usually when water flows gently over the edge of a pool, building it up by depositing calcite faster than it erodes it away. Calcite crystals sometimes form on dust particles on the water surface. In flowing water, these may form little discs that are supported by surface tension. In quieter waters, calcite can form entire sheets on the surface of the water. These are usually attached to the banks of the pool or any rock that protrudes from the water surface. The shelves remain in place when the water level drops, clearly indicating where previous water levels have remained stable for long periods.

■ **Cave pearls** form in water that moves but does not actively flow. These decorations, which form in depressions in the cave floor, consist of grains of sand or rock coated with calcite deposits.

■ There are many other minerals that cause cave formations. Aragonite is another mineral form of calcium carbonate that sometimes forms long needles and bunches of whiskers, while gypsum crystals form curls and twists known as **gypsum flowers**.

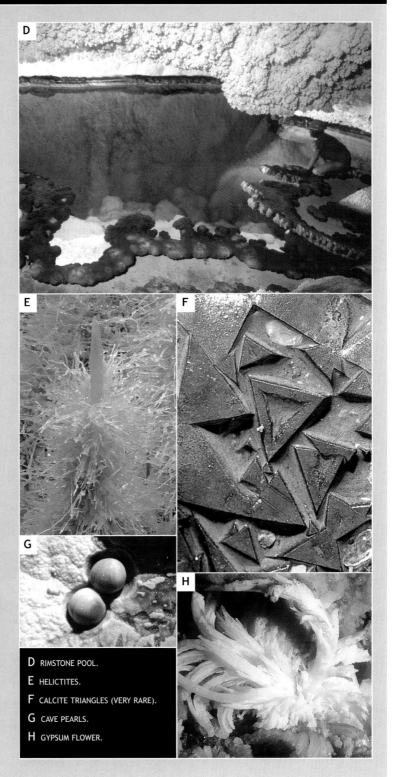

D RIMSTONE POOL.

E HELICTITES.

F CALCITE TRIANGLES (VERY RARE).

G CAVE PEARLS.

H GYPSUM FLOWER.

23

CAVES IN MANY PARTS OF THE WORLD ARE INHABITED BY BATS, NOCTURNAL ANIMALS THAT SWARM OUT TO FEED AT NIGHT. THEY PRESENT NO DANGER AND SHOULD NOT BE DISTURBED.

top A LONG-LEGGED CAVE CRICKET.

above BLIND CAVE FISH.

Just as varied as the processes that form caves are the splendid environments they produce and the highly specialized animals they frequently support. Together they create unique and very delicate ecosystems that must be respected and preserved.

Complete or partial darkness is the common denominator in all caves. The animals that live in this environment do not need direct sunlight to survive and have adapted to living in the dark by losing the features they no longer require, such as eyes and coloring. Instead, many species have developed other useful attributes like sensitive feelers and elongated legs that assist them in moving around and hunting for food.

While some of these animals spend their entire lives in the dark confines of caves, others — such as bats — use them to rest, but spend the remainder of their time outside and above ground.

The interesting creatures, the mysterious caves themselves and the splendid formations they contain are unique (calcite formations do occur on the surface but can never match the variety and density found underground).

While some caves are quite robust and able to withstand an enormous amount of disturbance before the natural balance of their ecosystems is disturbed, others are extremely delicate and cannot tolerate intrusions of any kind.

Each time a caver ventures underground, the cave he enters will change in some way. Each caver's challenge and duty, therefore, is to determine the correct balance between preserving the natural balance and the ability to explore and enjoy the beauty.

Most serious external threats, such as industry and development, are beyond the control of the average caver. Pollution, too, is a major concern since all water that flows through caves comes

IN THE SHELTERED ENVIRONMENT OF A CAVE, FOOTPRINTS WILL REMAIN ETCHED IN DUST OR MUD FOR MANY YEARS.

THOUGHTLESSLY DEFACED CAVE WALLS, ANOTHER FORM OF VANDALISM — SUCH GRAFFITI IS UNSIGHTLY AND DIFFICULT TO REMOVE.

from the surface and carries the pollutants it has picked up along the way into the cave. Building, mining and stone quarrying are further major threats (crushed limestone is extensively used for building and road construction).

The other, less-publicized threat — that caves are endangered by people, often cavers — is through thoughtless damage caused by carelessness and unnecessary pollution.

Erosion often occurs around heavy-traffic areas such as cave entrances where it is hardest to prevent. The lips of entrance pits are especially prone. Not only is the lip eroded, loose soil from the entrance may be washed into the cave after a heavy downpour causing the passages deeper down to silt up.

General wear and tear caused by cavers scraping along cave passages can do damage too.

Delicate crystals on the walls of narrow passages that carry a lot of cave traffic seldom last long.

The cave floor is the area that is damaged most often. A muddy boot carelessly placed can easily destroy a tiny, delicate formation, especially when the mud on the floor was that formation. Stalagmites often form on mud — one wrong step can derail a process that may have been underway for years. Carelessness is sad; wanton destruction unforgiveable! Never damage anything because you want a keepsake. Breaking pieces off formations is strictly taboo.

A sweet wrapper dropped on the way is unsightly, but unlikely to cause damage (this should, of course, not happen). Spent carbide discarded in a cave is a far more serious problem. It is not only unsightly, but a major pollutant. A discarded overall, caked in mud from a previous trip, gives

off clouds of fine dust that will dirty formations forever. Carbide lamps and tobacco smoke cause air pollution. Human waste is a serious problem. On short trips try to eliminate the need to have to relieve yourself in the cave. On longer trips ensure that all human waste is removed from the cave in sealed (and labelled) containers. Some kitty litter or a drying agent intended for use in chemical toilets can be added to the 'solids' container, as long as care is taken that none of the chemical is spilt in the cave.

Graffiti is associated with accessible caves that are popular with the public. Ranging from the odd initials scrawled in a corner to expansive murals, graffiti is an unsightly problem. In rare cases it can be removed, but this is time-consuming and expensive. Often the removal causes as much damage as the original defacing.

Caving Gear

in 1922, French speleologist Norbert Casteret was exploring the limestone region of the Pyrenees between France and Spain, when he came upon a resurgence near the village of Montespan. During this first exploration, Casteret simply undressed and took a deep breath before plunging into the dark, glacial waters. His second exploration was marginally more sensible, because he took along a few candles and matches, which he kept dry in a rubber bathing cap.

No more than bare essentials may have been enough to sustain Casteret during his epic five-hour journey into the icy gloom of the subterranean Pyrenees, but modern cavers should make use of the comfort offered by advanced technology, which ensures relatively warm bodies and reliable light sources.

Circumstances can vary dramatically from one cave to another. Being appropriately equipped for the exploration trip is essential for your enjoyment and, more importantly, your safe return to the outside world. It is difficult to decide which is more important — both clothing and lighting are vital as you would not get very far without them.

Protective clothing

The primary functions of protective clothing are to regulate body temperature and offer physical protection against abrasion. Whatever you decide to wear, remember that once it has been into a cave it will never look the same again.

Overheating can sometimes be a problem in warm, damp caves, but wet and cold conditions are far more common concerns facing the caver. This means that protective clothing should retain body heat and effectively repel water at the same time. Your clothing should never be bulky for it would make tight crawls difficult to negotiate; it should also not be too tight and restrictive so that you are still able to climb a rope or ladder comfortably and easily.

There is no universal coverall suitable for all caves you may encounter. Before you invest in specialized gear determine which type will suit your needs. Decide what type of cave interests you and how regularly you will go caving. If you wish to explore different cave environments you must consider investing in more than one type of caving suit. In cold and wet caves you will need clothing to keep you warm; in warm dry ones, where protection from abrasion is more important, any good-quality coverall will suffice.

Although denim jeans offer protection from scrapes and scratches they restrict movement, especially when you are crawling. Another disadvantage is that, once wet they take a long time to dry. This can become uncomfortable and cold and drain vital body heat. A good-quality synthetic coverall offers reasonable

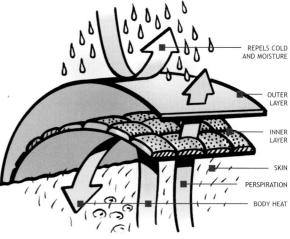

REPELS COLD AND MOISTURE

OUTER LAYER

INNER LAYER

SKIN

PERSPIRATION

BODY HEAT

above LAYERING PROVIDES THE BEST INSULATION. AN OUTER SHELL OF WATERPROOF MATERIAL REPELS COLD AND MOISTURE; THE INNER LAYER 'WICKS' PERSPIRATION AWAY FROM THE SKIN AND THROUGH THE OUTER LAYER, KEEPING THE BODY WARM AND DRY.

opposite WATER IS A COMMON FEATURE IN CAVES. GOOD, PROTECTIVE CLOTHING IS ESSENTIAL FOR MOST EXPEDITIONS AS A WET BODY COOLS DOWN QUICKLY, WHICH COULD RESULT IN HYPOTHERMIA.

Caving suits

A A FLUFFY, WARM UNDERSUIT MADE OF STRETCHABLE FIBER PILE, WITH ADDITIONAL KNEE PROTECTION. WEAR THIS UNDER THE COVERALL IN VERY COLD CAVES.

B SIMPLE, BOILER SUIT-TYPE COVERALL THAT IS REASONABLY ABRASION-RESISTANT.

C NYLON FABRIC, COATED WITH POLYURE-THANE TO MAKE IT WATERPROOF, FEATURING REINFORCED KNEES, SEAT AND A FOLD-AWAY HOOD IN THE COLLAR.

D PVC-COATED POLYESTER SUIT PERFECT FOR WET OR VERY MUDDY CAVES.

protection and dries out much faster, but ensure that it comes with a heavy-duty zip that will work even when it is caked in mud.

In most caves you will have to contend with water at some point. Even if you do not have to immerse yourself in it you may have to wade through a pool or duck under a waterfall. In warm, humid caves — especially those found in the tropics — water presents no danger, it is just uncomfortable. In all other caves, getting wet can be highly dangerous: it can lower body temperature and lead to hypothermia.

When you know that you will get a little wet, but not completely immersed in water, layering is the best approach. Layered clothing comprises an inner layer that provides thermal protection and a durable outer 'shell' that repels the odd splash or spray. A suitable outer layer would be a one-piece coverall made from a tough, abrasion-resistant material. Such fabric usually has a woven nylon or polyester base with a waterproof polyurethane or PVC (polyvinyl chloride) coating. Several brands of outer suits are available from caving equipment suppliers. If none of them are to your liking you could even make one yourself. Take special care when choosing zips, however. They should be of a good quality to ensure that they will still work efficiently even when they are clogged with mud.

The inner layer of the suit, also called the undersuit or 'furry', is designed to keep body heat in. It is made from a synthetic fiber such as polypropylene that keeps a layer of warm air trapped close to the skin. Even if it becomes saturated, the water drains quickly and the synthetic fiber of the undersuit should keep its structure and retain most of its insulating properties.

In a cave where you must dive or remain submerged in water for long periods, a good neoprene wetsuit with a thickness of at least 6mm (0.2in) will have to be worn. Do note, however, that one can get very cold in such a suit when one is not moving around; they can also cause severe overheating and exhaustion when one is not in water. Becoming increasingly popular are 3mm (0.1in) shortie wetsuits (arm protection up to the elbow and leg protection up to the knee) that can be worn under the coverall.

Socks

Although dedicated cavers spend much of their time underground suspended from ropes or crawling along narrow passages, their feet are still the major mode of transport. Very careful consideration must be given to comfortable socks and boots.

For general caving outings, ordinary woollen hiking socks will do adequately as they are cheap, warm and comfortable. Some cavers opt for the thicker neoprene variety that offers excellent protection in very cold and wet caving conditions. Made from the same material as wet suits, neoprene socks are much better at keeping your feet warm. The downside is that they tend to be more expensive than a pair of good-quality hiking socks.

Another very good option is waterproof socks made of a patented layered material that allows perspiration to escape without letting water in. These socks come with an elasticized waterproof band around the top, which seals against the leg and prevents water from spilling in. Waterproof socks can be over three times as expensive as woollen socks, however, and might be viewed as an unnecessary luxury item unless you are really serious about caving.

Remember to take along your socks when you go to buy your caving boots — their thickness could affect the size of boot you must choose.

A THICK PAIR OF HIKING SOCKS SHOULD KEEP YOUR FEET WARM AND COMFORTABLE ON MOST CAVING TRIPS. THEY ARE NOT WATERPROOF, HOWEVER, AND UNSUITABLE IN WET CAVES.

Boots

As with caving suits, the type of caving you do will determine the type of boot you should wear.

Hiking boots are designed to cope with the wear and tear of walking over uneven terrain. Caving boots must withstand much more than that, especially during crawls, when the toecaps — often covered in gritty, abrasive mud — are dragged over a rough cave floor.

Cheap rubber and fabric hiking boots, often designed for aesthetic appeal rather than durability, are not suitable. They are usually too soft, are not abrasion-resistant and provide very little protection.

In relatively dry caves, good-quality solid-leather hiking boots with a strong rubber sole will suffice. These are widely available, provide excellent ankle support and are relatively abrasion-resistant. Unfortunately, the more solidly constructed models are by far the heaviest — and when leather gets wet it becomes even heavier (it also takes a long time to dry). Attempting to dry leather boots by leaving them to bake in the sun is unwise. They usually become stiff in the process and the leather may crack. By quick-drying boots in this way you will make them uncomfortable to wear and shorten their life span.

For wet caves, rubber Wellington boots are a good choice. The standard garden variety is effective as long as the soles are not too flexible, otherwise they may get sucked off your feet in very muddy cave passages. An ankle-length, lace-up rubber boot is a solution to this problem. It laces across the top of the foot, making for a much more secure fit. The advantage of both types of boots is that they are quite cheap, virtually maintenance-free and able to withstand week after week of splashing through stream passages with hardly any care. Before you visit your local caving supplier, try to find an outlet that specializes in protective industrial gear. You may be able to buy exactly what you are looking for, but at a much better price.

A few cavers opt for plastic boots. Although originally designed for mountaineering in snow, they stand up very well to caving conditions. They are, however, more expensive than leather boots and available only from mountaineering suppliers.

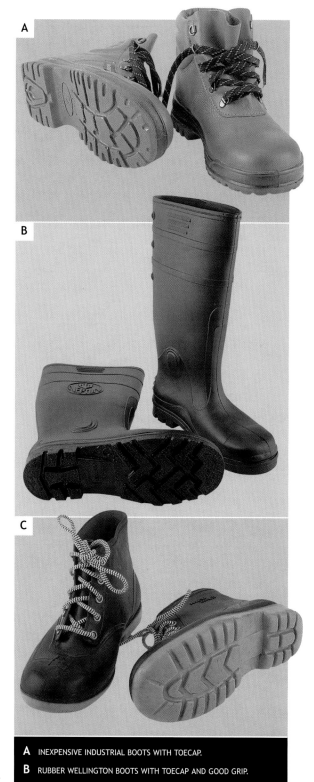

A INEXPENSIVE INDUSTRIAL BOOTS WITH TOECAP.

B RUBBER WELLINGTON BOOTS WITH TOECAP AND GOOD GRIP.

C ANKLE-HIGH LACE-UP BOOTS MADE OF RUBBER.

Tips on choosing caving boots

■ They must be large enough to accommodate your feet comfortably and securely, even when you are wearing a thick pair of hiking socks.

■ The rubber soles must be able to provide grip even in wet and muddy conditions.

■ Boots should provide ankle support without hindering flexibility of your foot.

■ Soles should neither be too stiff nor too flexible. Ordinary garden Wellington boots usually need a slightly stiffer sole.

■ Boots should be able to withstand extended wet periods without too much degradation.

■ They must be abrasion-resistant.

■ Lace-up models should not have hooks. Hooks can be extremely dangerous as they tend to get caught, especially on caving ladders.

■ Until you have decided on the ideal pair, army surplus boots will do for your first few trips. Remember to choose a pair that has combat soles, not drill soles which offer no grip.

Accessories

Cavers use their hands, knees and elbows as much as the soles of their feet, so ensure that these parts of the body are adequately protected for comfort, as well as for safety and unrestricted movement.

Gloves

Although some cavers dislike wearing them, gloves provide good protection and may improve grip.

■ For general caving, fabric or rubberized gardening gloves will do. Choose a type with fairly narrow or elasticized wrists as these are suitable for most purposes. Gloves with wide wrists tend to get caught in ropes or pulled off the hands. They also fill with water and dirt easily, which completely defeats their purpose.

■ Rubber, gauntlet-type gloves with reinforced hands are available from specialist shops and suppliers of industrial gear. These work well in muddy conditions but may make climbing and rope work difficult.

■ Cavers who do much ropework may be interested in special abseiling gloves. Made of leather, they feature reinforced patches stitched into the palm to protect the hands during fast rappelling.

Protective pads

In caves with long, low crawls, knees and elbows need additional protection. In such conditions, special elbow and knee pads are an important accessory.

■ Elbow pads are usually made from neoprene and slide over the arm like a supportive guard. For very long and very low crawls, elbow pads that extend down to cover the forearm offer even better protection.

■ Different models of knee pads are available; your choice depends on the type of caving you do and your personal preference. Neoprene guards slip over the legs. They cushion the knee during crawls along flat surfaces, but offer less protection on rocky ground.

For very rough, uneven surfaces, you may prefer knee guards with padded backing and a relatively stiff outer shell. They provide excellent protection from the hard cave floor. The downside is that mud and sand may get trapped between the straps and your skin when you are using the pads for an extended period, causing unpleasant chafing. They also restrict your movement and catch on rocks easily.

THREE DIFFERENT PAIRS OF GLOVES (FROM RIGHT TO LEFT): WIDE-WRIST LEATHER GLOVES NOT SUITABLE FOR ROPE WORK; GAUNTLET TYPE WITH REINFORCED HANDS; RUBBER GLOVES WITH ELASTIC WRIST BAND.

Helmets

Helmets are an essential part of protective gear and you should never go caving without one. The head is a very vulnerable part of the body and the dark environment of a cave holds many nasty surprises: whether you accidentally bang your head against the cave ceiling or are hit on the head by a falling rock, such incidents could necessitate a major rescue mission. Safety must always come first, so invest in a good head covering to prevent trauma.

Caving helmets have a hard outer shell that is usually made of carbon fiber, Kevlar™ or polycarbonate plastic and designed to prevent head injuries. The inner lining of the helmet is designed to fit snugly around the head and cushion it from contact with the hard outer shell. Two designs are used to manufacture inner liners and both are equally effective. In the one, the outer shell is filled with foam rubber (this can cause overheating), in the other with air. In the second type the shell is suspended above the head by a cradle of sturdy straps designed to absorb the impact of any object that falls onto the helmet. If you opt for the latter, avoid

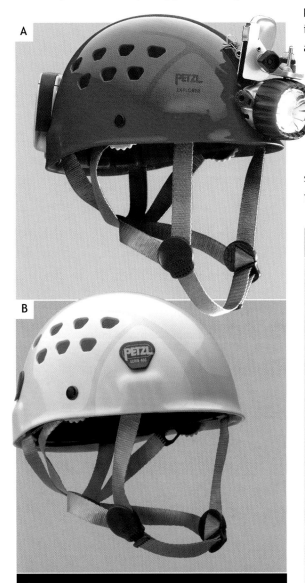

A A HELMET-MOUNTED LIGHTING COMBINATION IN ONE UNIT: CARBIDE LAMP AS PRIMARY LIGHT SOURCE, AS WELL AS LOW- AND HIGH-POWER ELECTRIC LAMPS.

B A MOUNTAINEER'S HELMET CAN BE USED FOR CAVING VENTURES IF IT IS FITTED WITH A LIGHTING SYSTEM.

Tips on choosing a helmet

■ A good caving helmet should be neither too loose nor too tight but should fit snugly and securely around your head. It must also come with a comfortable, adjustable chin strap.

■ Ensure that the chin strap is anchored to the helmet at four different points so the helmet is kept firmly on your head at all times.

■ Some customized caving helmets have built-in lights. If the helmet you want to buy does not have this feature, be sure to check that it has attachment points for headlamps.

■ Nothing should protrude into the inside of the helmet and the inner lining must be intact.

■ Beware of choosing a construction worker's helmet instead of investing in specialized caving headgear. It may be cheaper, but seldom comes with chin straps and can easily be knocked off just at the time when it is needed most. Another disadvantage is that this type of helmet has a built-in peak designed to shield the eyes from the glaring sun (unlikely in caves), which could severely restrict your vision in a low crawl.

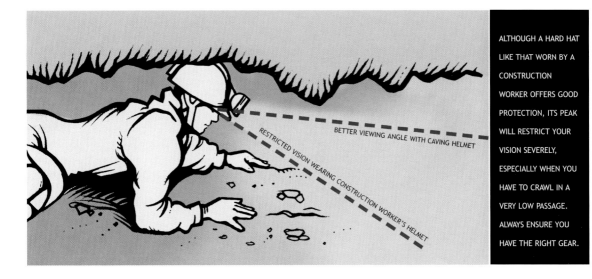

the temptation to use the air space between headband and hard outer shell for storing items like chocolate bars, spare batteries or space blankets. At the very low temperatures often encountered in caves a chocolate bar can harden substantially. If a sizeable rock lands on your helmet you may end up with a chocolate bar-shaped impression in your head at best — batteries are likely to do far more damage.

If you intend going on one or two easy, undemanding trips to familiarize yourself with caving and are unable to borrow a proper helmet, a construction worker's helmet is better than nothing at all. Do ensure that you fix a chin strap to it, however, and buy or borrow a head torch that can be strapped onto the helmet, rather than opt for the less reliable clip-on models. Use a few strips of duct tape to keep the straps in place and prevent them from sliding off.

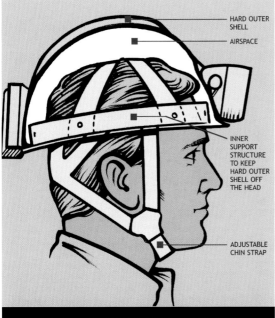

NEVER VENTURE BELOW GROUND WITHOUT THE APPROPRIATE HEAD PROTECTION. THE AIRSPACE ABOVE THE HEAD IS DESIGNED TO ABSORB AND DISSIPATE THE IMPACT OF A FALLING ROCK.

SOME MODERN HELMETS FEATURE BUILT-IN CLIPS THAT PROVIDE SECURE FASTENING FOR HEADLAMP STRAPS.

Lighting

Proper lighting is essential for safe caving. This means having a reliable lamp that is bright enough to navigate by and that will last for the duration of your intended trip. The wide range of technology and brands of lamps and torches available can make the choice confusing.

This section describes the different components of a lighting system and concludes by putting them together to create a functional system.

The first major choice you need to make is whether you prefer a conventional electrical lamp or a carbide model. Carbide lamps burn gas to give light, while the more familiar electrical torch uses a bulb to turn the chemical energy stored in batteries into light.

The carbide lamp

The energy for a carbide lamp is present in a chemical structure made of calcium carbide (a chemical compound containing calcium and carbon). When water is added to this calcium carbide compound a colorless and

PUT THE UNUSED CARBIDE INTO AN OLD SOCK BEFORE INSERTING IT INTO THE CARBIDE CHAMBER TO PREVENT CLOGGING.

Tips for using carbide lamps

■ Used carbide turns into an unappealing cream-colored wet sludge that is difficult to clean. If you insert the fresh carbide chips into an old sock before you load them into the gas generator, the spent carbide will be much easier to remove, and will also enable you to clean the generator easily and quickly.

■ If you are venturing into a dry cave, always remember to take water for yourself as well as for topping up your carbide lamp.

■ Never tip spent carbide in a cave or in water.

■ Take along a container for your spent carbide. This must not be airtight. Wet, spent carbide continues to produce acetylene gas which may explode if kept in a sealed container.

■ Always carry a thin wire to unclog the nozzle (plus a spare nozzle and the tools to fit it).

GAS PIPE

AIR BREATHER

WATER VALVE

WATER

ACETYLENE GAS

CARBIDE

THE PRINCIPLE OF ACETYLENE PRODUCTION IN A CARBIDE CHAMBER. CONTROLLED WATER FLOW ONTO THE CARBIDE GENERATES GAS.

near-odorless gas called acetylene is produced. (In reality, impurities in the carbide make this gas smell a little like aging garlic, which some cavers find so unpleasant that they prefer using electric lamps.) When acetylene is burned it gives off a bright soft light that is perfect for caving. Although carbide lamps have been around for a number of years, their fail-safe ease of use and excellent light quality makes them a popular choice even today.

Electric lamp systems

The energy for electric lamps is stored in a variety of cells. In very simple terms, a cell is a single unit that produces electricity – a number of such cells are combined to form a battery. There are two types of cells available: those that can be recharged repeatedly, and those that cannot and are thrown away.

Non-rechargeable cells are also called primary cells (not to be confused with the term 'primary caving lamp'). Their energy, once it has been used up, cannot be replenished and they must be discarded.

Rechargeable cells produce electrical current using a reversible chemical reaction. While the cells power a lamp, they are converting chemical energy into electrical energy.

When placed in a charger, the process is reversed and the cells convert electrical current from the charger back into stored chemical energy, ready to light the next caving trip. The process of extracting electricity and then recharging is known as a **charge-discharge cycle**.

The chemicals a cell uses to produce the reaction that will result in light determine not only its voltage and the amount of electrical energy that you will be able to extract from it; it also determines the number of charge-discharge cycles the cell can withstand, i.e. its total life span. This can range from as little as 50 cycles for alkaline cells, to over 2000 for nickel-cadmium cells, which obviously has price implications, so take care when you buy.

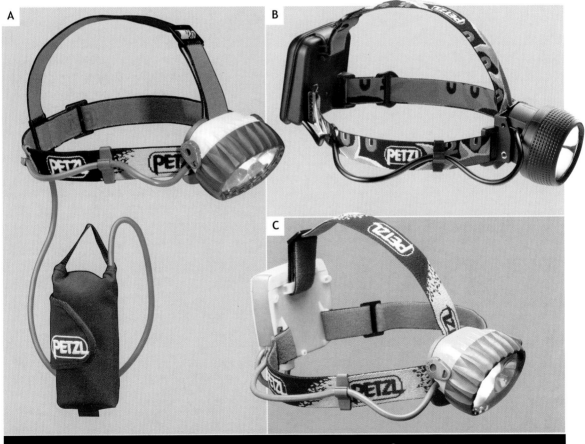

A A HEADLAMP POWERED BY A BELT-MOUNTED BATTERY PACK IN A POUCH.

B HEADLAMP FEATURING A HEAD-MOUNTED BATTERY PACK.

C WATERPROOF LIGHT WITH ZOOMABLE LAMP AND HEAD-MOUNTED BATTERY PACK.

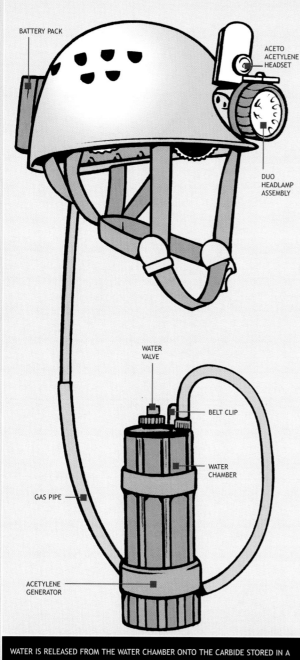

BATTERY PACK

ACETO
ACETYLENE
HEADSET

DUO
HEADLAMP
ASSEMBLY

WATER
VALVE

BELT CLIP

WATER
CHAMBER

GAS PIPE

ACETYLENE
GENERATOR

WATER IS RELEASED FROM THE WATER CHAMBER ONTO THE CARBIDE STORED IN A SEPARATE COMPARTMENT BELOW. GAS IS RELEASED, WHICH ESCAPES THROUGH THE NARROW PIPE THAT FEEDS INTO THE HEAD-MOUNTED LAMP. HERE THE GAS BURNS WITH AN OPEN FLAME TO GIVE OFF A BRIGHT LIGHT.

Due to the trade-offs in lamp life, brightness and reliability, no one torch is able to meet all of a caver's lighting needs. To get around this dilemma, most cavers either carry more than one torch lamp, or invest in a multi-function torch designed to fulfil more than one need.

A caver's **primary lamp** is switched on before going into the cave and often switched off only on leaving the cave again. The primary lamp must be helmet-mounted for optimal use, and should be strong enough to safely light your entire subterranean trip.

Many cavers still use carbide as their primary light, but electric lamps are less messy and fast gaining in popularity.

If you are using an electric system remember that it should provide you with at least six to eight hours of continuous light on a single charge or set of batteries, and use a 2W (watt) bulb. The strength of light is a matter of personal taste, but the general rule is: the brighter the better. Some cavers are happy with 1W while others will not venture underground with less than 4W.

The headsets of many caving lamps are fitted with two bulbs and a three-position switch (on/off, normal and high beam). The high beam, usually activated by a powerful 6W halogen bulb, is usually used for short periods and only when a much brighter beam is needed. There are several commercial dual-bulb lighting systems available from specialist suppliers, but some very robust dual models can be bought from mining suppliers.

A recent innovation are caving lamps using clusters of LEDs (light-emitting diodes) to provide light. A useful feature that was designed to save the life of a battery is that some of the LEDs can be switched off or electronically dimmed whenever bright light is not required. One particular commercially available LED model, which runs on a lithium battery, even features sophisticated electronics that actually extend the life of the battery. It is able to provide up to an impressive 50 hours of light when set in the normal-beam mode and up to 12 hours on the high-beam setting.

A POWERFUL HALOGEN BULB SURROUNDED BY POWER-SAVING LEDs.

The only real disadvantage of LED bulbs is that they come with a built-in lens, which makes it virtually impossible to change their focus. What this means is, that if you want the reliability of an LED lamp, but do sometimes prefer the long-distance power and range of a halogen light, you will have to consider investing in two separate lamps.

One manufacturer has solved this problem by producing a head-lamp featuring a halogen main beam srrounded by a number of LEDs. This headlamp, readily available from caving supply specialists, is popular with cavers worldwide.

Battery positions

To ensure optimal long-life performance, some batteries come with a large battery pack that has to be clipped onto a belt.

The cable running between pack and headlamp can be quite cumbersome as it often twists around the body and tends to get snagged on rocks.

Some high-capacity batteries are lightweight enough to be worn on the helmet. When they are positioned on the back of the helmet they balance the weight on the front, but the additional protrusion can prove to be a hindrance in low crawls. If you do opt for such a battery pack, ensure that it is not too heavy for you or you may develop an unpleasant headache.

Battery packs mounted on the front of helmets were originally designed for fishing, hiking and general outdoor use. They are inexpensive and make useful backup lights.

LARGE BELT-MOUNTED BATTERY PACKS PROVIDE MORE POWER FOR A CAVER'S HEADLAMP, BUT ARE CLUMSY.

RECHARGE HELMET-MOUNTED BATTERY PACKS BY SLIDING OUT THE CASING AND REPLENISHING IT WITH FRESH BATTERIES.

Non-rechargeable cells and batteries

TYPE	BENEFITS	DRAWBACKS	COMMENTS
Zinc-carbon 1.5V AA cell	Cheap Steep discharge curve	Very low energy density, so does not last long	Not suitable for caving
Alkaline 1.5V AA Cells	Readily available Sloping discharge curve, but good as backup High energy density (200 per cent more than zinc-carbon) Shelf life of over three years — can be left in the bottom of your pack for emergencies	Expensive option — a new set is required for each caving trip	Useful for backup lights
Alkaline 1.5V D cells	Higher energy density than AA cells	Too heavy for helmet mount	Mainly used for hand torches, not headlamps
Alkaline 4.5V battery	Easy to replace in the cave High energy density	Not always easily available	About the right size to mount on a helmet Same voltage, but much longer life than three AA batteries
Lithium 3V cell	High energy density (40 per cent more than alkaline cell)	Expensive Steep discharge curve	Excellent life span when used together with electronics that give a constant light output

Rechargeable cells and batteries

TYPE	BENEFITS	DRAWBACKS	COMMENTS
Lead acid battery (2V per cell)	Easily available Provides a constant light output	Very heavy Less than 100 charge-discharge cycles	Cannot fast-charge (use constant voltage charger) Don't store when discharged
Alkaline 1.5V AA rechargeable	Direct replacement for primary alkaline cell	Constant voltage charger required Less than 30 charge-discharge cycles	Its voltage makes this a direct replacement for normal AA cells Limited number of cycles means they are expensive
NiCad 1.2V AA cell	Cheap (and cheap chargers) Long cell life (2000 charge cycles) Reasonable energy density	Need to discharge before recharging, due to memory effect (see page 92)	Popular; charge evening before as NiCads lose 8–10 per cent charge a week
NiCad 1.2V F cell	Higher energy density than AA NiCad cell	Not always available individually	Popular in a commercially available battery pack
NiMH 1.2V AA cell	Relatively cheap 50 per cent more energy than equivalent NiCad No memory effect when charging	About half the recharge cycles of NiCad	Replacement for NiCad Can fast-charge (but be sure to charge evening before. Goes flat easily when left standing) Rapid self-discharge
Li-Ion 3.6V cell	Has double the energy density of a NiCad	Steep discharge slope Electronics required	Can fast-charge (special charger required)

Lighting supply checklist

The following checklist highlights the key factors a caver should consider when choosing a particular type of cell or battery.

■ Will it produce enough **energy** to light the entire caving trip? The amount of energy in a cell is referred to as energy density (normally quoted in milli-amp hours, or mAhr). The higher the energy density, the longer the light will last.

■ Will the light be bright enough? The **brightness** is determined by strengths of the light bulb and the batteries.

■ Determine the **reliability** by assessing the discharge curve. Will the light be consistently bright throughout, or fade dramatically halfway through or towards the end of your trip? The voltage printed on the side of a cell is called the nominal voltage. As soon as you attach a light bulb the cell's voltage drops. The rate at which it does this is called the discharge curve.

A flat discharge curve means that light produced will stay reasonably constant, while a steeply sloping discharge curve indicates that the light will dim faster.

■ **Weight** should be considered. Are the cells light enough to carry comfortably? This matters less when they are going to be mounted on the belt, but if they are going to be mounted on your helmet, take weight into consideration.

■ Will the cell be reliable at a low **temperature**? Some caves can be very cold indeed and certain battery types cease to function when the temperature drops below a certain level.

■ **Size** is important in determining which cell will be the most economical for you to use. As a rule, bigger cells have a higher energy density than smaller ones as long as their chemical make-up is identical. This means that an alkaline cell of 4.5V, i.e. three times the size of a 1.5V alkaline cell, will produce more than three times the energy released by the smaller one.

CLEVER LIGHTING REVEALS THE SPECTACULAR GLORY OF THIS LARGE UNDERGROUND CHAMBER OF A CAVE IN BELIZE, CENTRAL AMERICA.

Bulbs

A bulb is the part of the lamp that turns electrical energy into light. Although light output is correctly measured in lumens, most cavers refer to the amount of light a bulb can produce by stating the amount of electrical energy it consumes. Quoted in watts (W) this gives a reasonable approximation when comparing one bulb to another.

The most common type of bulb comprises a small tungsten filament inside a glass bulb. As electric current passes through the filament it heats up and gives off light. Ordinary filament bulbs are used for general lighting while travelling through a cave.

Halogen bulbs are filled with a special gas that allows a much higher current to flow through the filament. This results in a brighter light, but also means an increased energy consumption. The strong light generated by halogen bulbs is used in special lamps designed to illuminate long passages or probe the lofty ceiling of a high chamber.

Fluorescent lamps produce bright light by exciting a layer of phosphor. This process is much more efficient than the heating of a filament in a glass tube; the disadvantage is that it requires electronics to generate the high voltage needed to excite the phosphor. A few commercial caving lights do feature fluorescent tubes but these are not commonly used.

LEDs are solid-state electronic lamps. They are relatively new to cavers as manufacturers have only recently been able to produce LEDs bright enough for use in this specialized environment.

Despite technological advances, one LED is still not sufficient for a caver's needs (these lamps generally use between seven and 48 LEDs clustered together). As manufacturers continue to refine their products in an effort to improve the light output, this number is expected to drop.

A   B

A   BUILT INTO LAMPS, LEDs ARE RELIABLE BUT CANNOT BE REPLACED.

B   A HIGH-POWER QUARTZ HALOGEN BULB PROVIDES BRIGHT LIGHT.

BULB TYPE	BENEFITS	DRAWBACKS	COMMENTS
Ordinary (traditional) filament	Cheap, normal light	Relatively fragile filament Inefficient when dimmed	This is used as the primary source of light for most caving trips
Halogen	Very bright light	Uses much more energy, so the battery will not last as long Inefficient when dimmed	Used as a temporary light to illuminate distant objects
Fluorescent	Efficient	Requires electronics Difficult to focus Expensive	Not commonly used, but quite efficient Gives a flattish light
White LEDs	Very long bulb life LEDs will usually outlast the rest of the lamp They can be dimmed very efficiently	Low output means a whole cluster is required for adequate light (can be costly) Some cavers do not like white light	Gives pure white light Sometimes flattish light

Distance in meters (m)	0	20	40	60	80
CARBIDE					
NORMAL BEAM 2W					
HALOGEN BEAM 6W ZOOMED					
LED LAMP					

LIGHTING SYSTEMS HAVE DIFFERENT CHARACTERISTICS AND STRENGTHS. THIS CHART COMPARES THE AVERAGE DISTANCE LIT UP BY THE FOUR MAIN TYPES.

NORMAL, HALOGEN AND LED LAMPS PRODUCE BEAMS, WHILE CARBIDE CREATES A SPHERE OF SOFT LIGHT.

Backup lights

Apart from a primary light, cavers should also carry at least one, but preferably two, backup lights. Consider the following when you pack your caving bag:

■ Some headlamps, intended for anglers and hikers, are quite cheap so there is absolutely no excuse for not taking a backup lamp along.

■ The backup should provide as much light as your primary caving light (about 2W).

■ It must last long enough to get you out of the cave in the event that your primary light fails.

■ If you do a lot of ropework, ensure that a backup light is mounted on your helmet. If your main lamp fails while you are halfway up a pitch it may be impossible for you to retrieve the spare lamp from your bag.

■ Always carry spare batteries with you. You should have enough to last at least twice the intended length of your caving trip.

■ Always take spare bulbs with you (both for the normal and the main beam).

■ Always keep a candle and a lighter in a sealed plastic bag at the bottom of your pack for use in dire emergencies.

BE SURE THAT YOUR BATTERY PACK IS WATERPROOF OR YOU MAY RUN INTO TROUBLE (AND OUT OF LIGHT) IN WET CAVES.

Getting Started

exploration of a cave can present enormously varied challenges. An outing could include a gentle amble down a wide flat passage, a wet and muddy crawl up to the eyebrows in water, an easy scramble up a slope and hanging precariously from the end of a rope over a yawning chasm. Technique is the key element that will allow you to negotiate all these obstacles, enjoy the wonders of the underground wilderness and return safely to the surface.

Horizontal techniques

Even if a passage is wide and high enough to allow you to walk at a good pace, always concentrate on where you put your feet. Safety must be your prime concern, so look where you are going. Cavers often encounter obstacles where they least expect them – they may overlook a rock in the path, stumble and fall, or the cave floor may suddenly vanish into a deep pit. Injuries sustained far from the entrance of a cave could turn an outing into a serious nightmare for the entire team.

Coping with low passages

In very low cave passages you will have to stoop. If you are forced to proceed like this over lengthy distances you could experience backache, especially when you are carrying a heavy bag. Avoid pain by straightening your back every now and again, even if it means squatting or sitting down.

When the passage gets too low you will have to crawl. This is where gear such as thick leather gloves, knee pads and a peakless helmet are useful. The helmet will let you see the passage ahead without having to tilt your head too far back (*see page 33*) and padding will protect you from the floor.

Try not to drag your legs on the ground, but lift them clear off the cave floor as you move forward. Dragging your feet will wear away the toes of your boots and create friction that will tire you quickly.

In exceptionally low passages your only option is to lie flat on your stomach and pull yourself along. Once again, avoid dragging yourself along as this creates unnecessary friction. Instead, lift your body as much as you can before maneuvering arms and legs forward. You may also have to remove your helmet and turn your head sideways to fit through. If you are forced to do this, push your helmet ahead of you, turning the light away from your face. Beware of pushing the helmet so far forward that you cannot reach it anymore.

Avoiding obstacles

When you are crawling along a passage, you can avoid any protrusion or puddle you encounter by hovering over it in a press-up position. You need very good upper body strength to do this as your body weight will have to be supported on your hands and toes while moving forward. Obviously, this technique is only effective if the passage is high and wide enough. Once you have mastered it, however, you will be able to avoid a variety of smaller obstacles.

Negotiating narrow passages

When you are pulling yourself forward in a low, narrow passage, try not to get your elbows trapped too far behind your shoulders. There is a chance that you will pull yourself forward and end up lying on your arms. The narrow passage will prevent you from moving your elbows out to free your arms, while the low ceiling will prevent you from lifting yourself up. Avoid this situation by keeping at least one arm extended in front of you at all times. Your progress will seem slower, but the chances of getting stuck are greatly reduced.

opposite IN A TIGHT CRAWL THROUGH A LOW, WATER-FILLED PASSAGE REMOVE YOUR HELMET, POINTING THE LIGHT AWAY FROM YOUR FACE SO THAT IT DOES NOT BLIND YOU, AND PROCEED CAREFULLY.

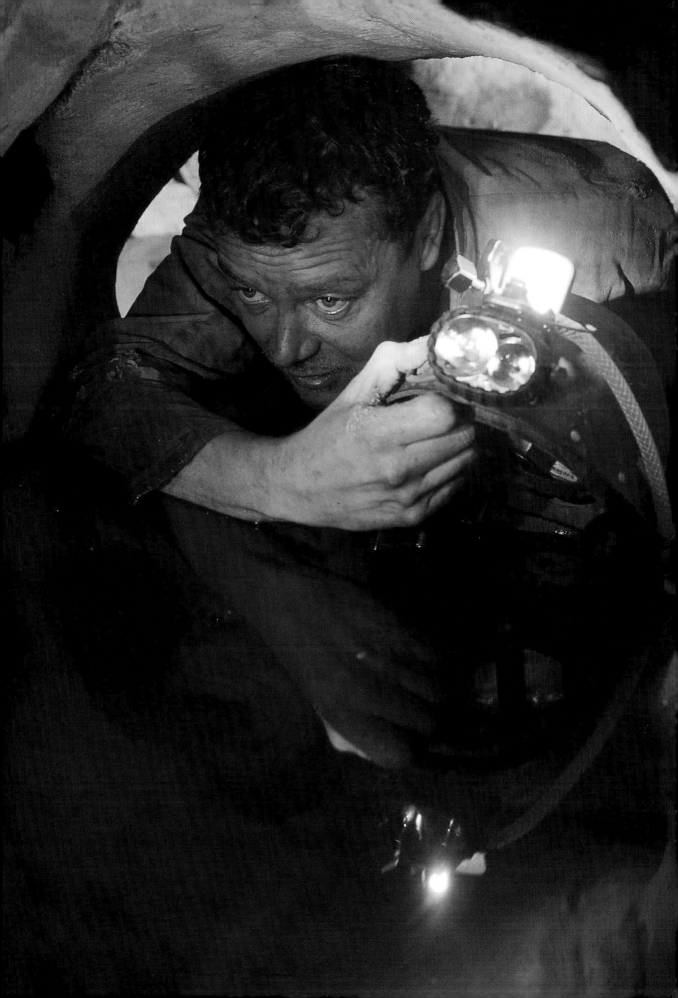

Getting stuck

Every novice caver fears the possibility of getting stuck in a small space, unable to get out. These tips will teach you how to handle the situation.

■ Don't panic. Getting out will require focused thought, so keep your wits about you and try to remain calm.

■ Don't fight the rock. It will always win. If you are jammed into a narrow section, pushing and shoving wildly will sap your energy, could cause an injury and may serve to wedge you in even more.

■ Relax, lie still and breathe evenly until you have calmed down enough to proceed.

■ Inch your way back the way you came even if it means moving only a fraction at a time.

■ Ensure that you do not flare your elbows out to the sides. This would hinder your progress.

■ Ask the person behind you to grab onto your feet. They may not possess the strength to pull you out, but it could be helpful if you have something to pull, or lever against in order to try and inch your way forward.

■ Ask the person behind you to tug down your trouser legs. When you maneuver backward in a narrow passage, your trouser legs may catch against the wall and bunch up painfully between your legs. A gentle tug from behind will prevent this and also help to reduce friction between your trousers and the cave walls.

Moving in water

Water in caves can be extremely dangerous and must always be treated with caution, especially when it is flowing swiftly, because the power of the current could easily sweep you off your feet.

If you have to cross an underground river or move along a stream passage that is filled with deep, flowing water, it is wise to attach a rope to your body and have someone else belay you to safety from the bank. (*See* page 46 for belaying.)

Sump is the caving term used to describe the point at which the water in a passage meets a very low cave ceiling, thus filling the passage completely and flooding it. Some sumps are only a few centimeters long, but you may encounter underwater stretches of a considerable distance. Submerged stretches measuring less than 1m (3ft) are sometimes known as 'ducks' (note, however, that in the UK this term describes a water-filled passage with an airspace).

It is impossible to estimate the length of unfamiliar sumps without entering and surveying their underwater course — a task best left to experienced cavers. This

INCORRECT TECHNIQUE WILL RESULT IN BOTH ARMS BEING WEDGED USELESSLY UNDER A CAVER'S BODY. IF THIS HAPPENS TO YOU: DO NOT PANIC AND WIGGLE AROUND WILDLY. REMAIN CALM, BREATHE EVENLY AND THINK LOGICALLY.

makes them potentially very dangerous. Avoid them unless you know exactly how long they are and that they may be negotiated safely.

Never hold your breath, but exhale while you are moving through a sump. Also remember that the fine silt in cave rivers is easily stirred up, this will blur your vision if you are diving with your eyes open and can also cause serious disorientation.

Vertical cracks

A vertical crack is a passage that is higher than it is wide. Cross sections have revealed that vertical cracks are often diamond-shaped: narrow and pointed at the top and bottom, and wide in the middle. Moving through such a difficult passage can be extremely tiring.

Unlike a crawl in a horizontal crack where you can rest simply by stopping and lying where you are, resting in a vertical passage could result in a plunge down into the crack where — even if you survive the fall — you could get seriously stuck.

If you do need to rest, try to remain in the widest section in the middle of the passage. Rest your arms by breathing in and spreading out your body as much as you can. This should wedge you firmly in place and take the strain off your arms.

In vertical cracks that are wide but have a very narrow bottom section, it is sometimes easier to 'walk' along the walls. To do this, find a section where the walls are a comfortable distance apart and move along with one foot and supporting arm placed on either side of the wall. Only attempt this if you are wearing boots with good non-slip soles, or you could fall and injure yourself. If the crack is very high, beware of going too far up — you run the risk of slipping and plummeting to the bottom of the crack.

A TIGHT VERTICAL CRACK REQUIRES CONCENTRATION, TECHNIQUE AND GOOD NERVES. BY EXTENDING HIS LOWER ARM IN FRONT OF HIM, THIS CAVER WILL BE ABLE TO SLIDE THROUGH THE NARROW GAP.

ASCEND A VERTICAL CRACK THAT IS WIDE ENOUGH TO ACCOMMODATE YOU COMFORTABLY BY SPREAD-EAGLING YOUR BODY AND CLIMBING WITH LIMBS PLACED SECURELY ON EITHER SIDE.

Vertical techniques

Not all caving is horizontal; some of the most exciting maneuvers involve dangling at the end of a rope. The use of ropes in caving is known as Single Rope Technique (SRT), covered in more detail in Chapter 5.

For obvious reasons, expeditions that require you to negotiate large vertical drops are more dangerous than horizontal caving. Before you venture into any cave, it is wise to join an organized club in your area so that you can learn from experienced cavers.

A little rock climbing experience will not prepare you adequately for the rigours of caving. While there are similarities between the two, the dark, confined environment of caves makes movement much more difficult. For this reason, you must learn correct rope technique and focus on the importance of safety whenever you go caving.

Belaying

Belaying can mean different things: it refers to the practice of attaching a rope firmly to a rock or a cave wall to act as an anchor, but is also used to describe a rope that runs between two cavers to protect them from falling down while climbing up.

In short, a caver who is being belayed while climbing a dangerous or exposed section usually wears a sit harness that has a rope attached to it. The person at the other end (the belayer) ensures that a sling of this rope is firmly anchored and that a friction device is attached to the anchor. The belayer 'feeds' the rope, protecting and controlling the climber's descent by means of a friction device. (The friction is adjusted by changing the angle of the rope where it feeds into the device.)

The belayer, too, should be firmly attached to a solid anchor so that neither caver is pulled off the edge of the pitch. The belayer gives the climber enough slack to enable him to move with ease while keeping the rope as taut as possible.

Should a climber accidentally fall, the friction device would lock to prevent or slow the fall. In the event of a fall, ensure that you have enough rope, so that you can be lowered to safety or a position from where you can rescue yourself and your partner.

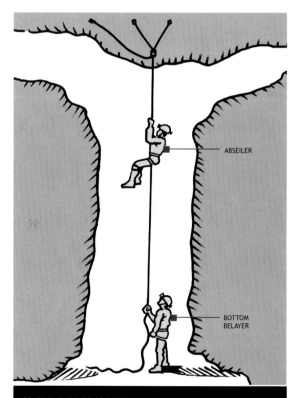

ABSEILER

BOTTOM BELAYER

A CAVER BELAYS HIS DESCENDING FRIEND FROM ABOVE, FEEDING HIM ROPE THROUGH A BELAY BRAKE ANCHORED TO A SOLID ROCK FEATURE.

CONTROL THE RATE OF DESCENT OF AN ABSEILER BY REGULATING THE TENSION OF THE ROPE: PULLING DOWN WILL STOP HIM.

WHEN YOU DESCEND INTO A CAVE, ENSURE THAT NOTHING CAN HAMPER YOUR PROGRESS OR ENDANGER YOU IN ANY WAY. THIS CAVER LETS HIS TACKLE BAG DANGLE SAFELY OUT OF THE WAY BELOW HIM DURING HIS DESCENT.

Ladders

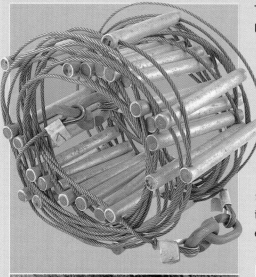

The advance of caving ladders revolutionized vertical caving. Very popular when first introduced, they have lost appeal in recent years since cavers discovered the challenges of skillful rope technique. Ladders still have their place in caving, however, especially on short pitches where it often takes less time to get a group of cavers up a ladder than it would using SRT ropes only.

Caving ladders are generally made only in short lengths. They have aluminium rungs strung securely between two strands of galvanized steel cable. Lengths are designed in such a way that they can be joined together easily to make them more versatile.

above A LADDER ALLOWS ACCESS TO DEEP PARTS OF A CAVE.

top A ROLLED-UP CAVING LADDER.

Tips on rigging a ladder

On a caving outing you need to decide on the most suitable place to position (rig) a ladder so that cavers can use it safely. When rigging a ladder, you should:

■ Check the safety of the position so that cavers can get on and off easily. If possible, attach it above the step-on point so it doesn't move to and fro and cavers have a secure stance before they begin to climb.

■ Avoid running a ladder along the cave floor or directly over the edge of a pit.

■ Select a position where the ladder does not twist or is in danger of getting wedged in cracks as this will make climbing very difficult. The ladder should ideally hang freely down into the pitch.

■ Choose a sturdy safe anchor, such as a protruding rock or conveniently placed bolt, to attach the ladder in such a way that it cannot damage the cave.

■ Ensure that rungs cannot get snagged on projecting rocks. Not only could this damage the ladder, it can be very dangerous. If one rung has become snagged on a sharp rock, the caver would have to place his full weight on the one immediately above or below to steady himself. This may bend or even break the rung.

Ladder climbing made easy

Climbing a caving ladder requires a little practice, but is quite easy once you have mastered it.

These practical hints should make your first attempts on the ladder less laborious and safer:

■ Before you get onto a ladder, ensure that you are securely belayed from above.

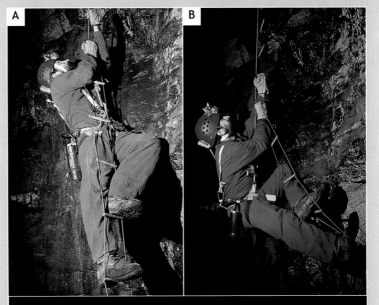

A CORRECT LADDER TECHNIQUE: THE LEGS AND FEET DO ALL THE WORK IN ASCENDING THE LADDER WHILE THE ARMS ARE USED PURELY TO KEEP THE CLIMBER UPRIGHT AND MAINTAIN A VERTICAL POSITION.

B THE INCORRECT WAY TO CLIMB A LADDER: NOTICE HOW THE CLIMBER'S LEGS SWING OUT TO THE FRONT BECAUSE HE IS USING HIS ARMS TO CLIMB. AS A RESULT HIS POSITION IS INSECURE, UNSTABLE AND TIRING.

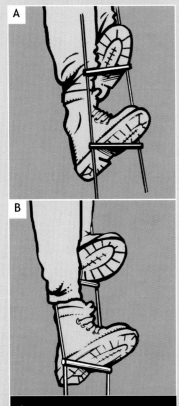

A THE CONVENTIONAL WAY OF CLIMBING A LADDER ALLOWS FOR A SWIFT ASCENT OR DESCENT. THE CLIMBER'S FEET STEP ONTO THE RUNGS FROM THE FRONT.

B FOR A MORE BALANCED CLIMB THE LEG IS WRAPPED AROUND SO THAT YOU STEP ONTO THE RUNG HEEL FIRST.

■ Aim to maintain your center of gravity directly above your feet at all times. This means you will climb primarily with your feet, using your arms only to keep yourself upright.

■ Using your arms to climb will not only exhaust you much quicker, it will also make your climbing movements inefficient as your feet will end up sticking out in front of you.

■ There are two ways of climbing a ladder — simply putting your feet onto the rungs from the front, or wrapping one or both legs around the back and climbing on the heels of your boots. Either method is effective as long as the ladder is not touching a wall and hangs freely down into the shaft.

■ Climbing up or down becomes a great deal trickier when the ladder rests against a slope.

The rungs are usually no more than 12–15mm (0.5–0.6in) in diameter. When they rest against a rockface there is not much space left to stand on. In this case, the best measure is to climb by turning the ladder so that its rungs are perpendicular to the wall, or use your boot as a spacer to keep the ladder away from it.

Learning the Ropes

descending into deep, sheer vertical pits is one of the most thrilling aspects of caving. Rope work is what allows cavers to do this. It is also a learned skill — one that is acquired only through dedicated practice.

Beginners are not advised to experiment with ropes under any circumstances, unless they have undergone prior training. One slip or wrong move could be fatal. You cannot rely on books to learn rope technique; it is much more sensible to join an organized caving club in your area. Ensure that you have an experienced and qualified instructor who can teach you how to use ropes properly and safely.

Single rope technique

In order to further their exploration cavers began to descend deeper and deeper into the bowels of the earth, and the heavy, unwieldy ladders they had used up until then became less and less attractive.

Single Rope Technique (SRT) was the answer to their problem. In SRT a rope is firmly attached to a strong anchor point (such as a protruding rock or bolt) located near the lip of a pit. It is then lowered or threaded down the pitch in such a way that it touches the rock in as few places as possible. Cavers use special devices known as descenders to abseil down the rope to the bottom of the pitch. In order to get up again, cavers attach devices known as ascenders to climb the rope.

Properties of ropes

Climbers use ropes to protect themselves in the event of a fall. Also known as dynamic ropes, they are designed to absorb the impact of a fall by stretching.

The ropes used in SRT have very different properties from the ones used by mountain and sport climbers. An SRT rope is used like a ladder and must have as little stretch as possible (static rope). Good-quality static ropes have a very high breaking strain and will be able to lift about 3048kg (3 tons). They are often white or green, but do not take color as your guide — always tell the supplier that you require a static rope for SRT and caving (11mm or 13mm; 0.4in or 0.5in is a good choice for a main SRT rope on a long pitch).

Proper rope care

- Treat with care, your life depends on them.
- Never stand on them. Grit clinging to the soles of your boots will damage them.
- Clean after use. Grit in the fibres will chafe the inside of the rope every time it is flexed.
- Inspect for damage regularly. If a rope shows signs of damage, do not use it.
- Do not use chemicals to clean. Carefully read and follow instructions on accompanying leaflet.
- Don't use to tow cars or for any other purpose.
- Store in clean, dry and dark environment.
- Keep ropes separate from other equipment in their own tackle bags.

opposite ROPE WORK IS AN ESSENTIAL COMPONENT OF CAVING. YOU MUST LEARN TO ASCEND AND DESCEND WITH CONFIDENCE.

Sailors were long considered the knot experts of the world as much of their time was spent working with ropes. Mountaineers took over many of their knots and developed new ones. Austrian climber Karl Prusik even developed a knot (named after him) especially for climbing up ropes.

Only some of these are used in caving, but all share a common principle: a length of rope is tied to itself, another rope, or an object (anchor rock or bolt) in such a way that the resulting friction in the loops prevents it from opening and provides a very secure fastening instead.

Knotting a rope does reduce its strength, so avoid tying too many knots too often. However, a good knot that is easy to tie and quickly undo will not reduce the strength too much.

Serious cavers must know many knots. For the beginner, a few very basic ones will do.

Figure 8

Versatile, strong, and very easy to tie and untie even when it has been put under great strain, a single figure 8 is a good stop knot at the end of a rope to prevent you from abseiling off the end. It can also form the start of a double figure 8 when it is tied around itself or onto something else.

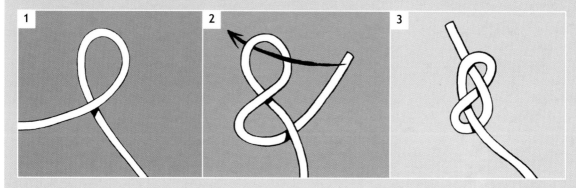

Double figure 8

This double figure 8 is tied on a bight (a piece of rope folded in on itself, or in the middle of a rope). Its double strands give it a characteristic shape that stands out well and is quick to spot and check even in the poor light of a cave. Simple to tie, it is not so easily undone, especially when wet.

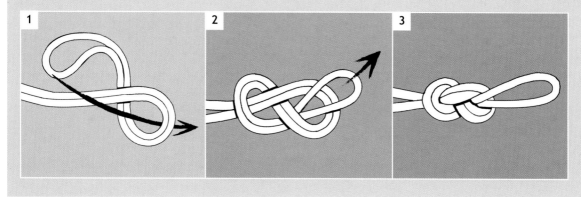

Bowline with half hitch

The bowline (1–3) is a versatile general-purpose knot, easy to untie after it has been loaded (so easy, in fact, that its short end may work loose of its own accord). To prevent this, always secure it with one or two half hitches (4). Another disadvantage is that it tends to weaken the rope, more so than a figure 8.

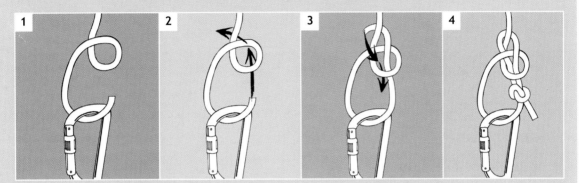

Alpine butterfly

The alpine butterfly creates a loop in the middle of a rope while keeping the direction of the rope in a straight line. It is easy to tie and very useful, as strain can be applied on either side of the knot.

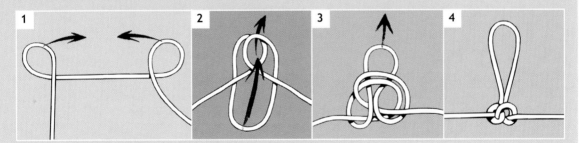

The Italian hitch

This useful emergency knot can be used to create friction if you have to belay a fellow caver without an appropriate belaying device. Note that the Italian hitch can be reversed to yield slack or apply tension, simply by taking the strain off the loaded rope and asserting it on the braking rope.

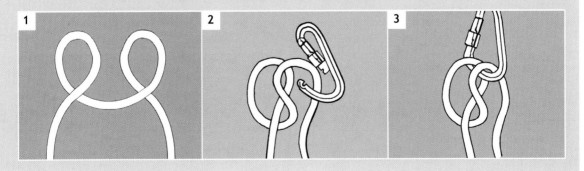

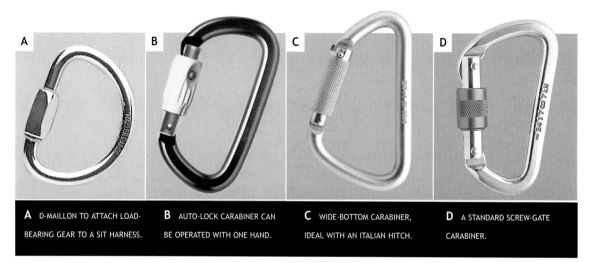

A D-MAILLON TO ATTACH LOAD-BEARING GEAR TO A SIT HARNESS.

B AUTO-LOCK CARABINER CAN BE OPERATED WITH ONE HAND.

C WIDE-BOTTOM CARABINER, IDEAL WITH AN ITALIAN HITCH.

D A STANDARD SCREW-GATE CARABINER.

Carabiners

Carabiners, also called snaplinks, are metal clips made of steel or aluminium that are used to join ropes and slings together. They are roughly oval in shape and have a hinged gate on one side that allows this device to be connected to the middle of a rope, or through a loop in an anchor. The gate makes the carabiner easy to use, but is also its weakest part.

Designed for improved safety and security, a screw-gate carabiner features a threaded cylinder that can be screwed tight to lock the gate. Another version replaces the threaded cylinder and has a spring-loaded device that allows the user to open, close and lock the carabiner with only one hand.

A maillon rapide is a special link that does not have a hinged gate but is closed using a threaded cylinder. The cylinder is screwed securely onto both ends of the opening, making the link very strong. The disadvantage of maillons is that they require both hands and considerably more time to put in place.

Never load a carabiner along its short axis. When loaded along its long axis, a carabiner can hold about 2500kg (5510lb), but usually less than half this amount along its short axis.

Bolts and hangers

When ropes have to be firmly attached to rock for safety reasons and natural anchors are unavailable, bolts have to be used. Unless you are using an 8mm self-drill anchor bolt, or a resin anchor inserted into a hole drilled with a battery operated drill, you will have to use a special electric rock drill or a hand drill to create a hole for an expansion bolt. Ensure that depth and diameter of the hole are correct so that the bolt fits in tightly and securely, or it will be unsafe to use.

Insert and slide the bolt through the hole in the hanger before tightening it. This will cause it to expand and grip the rock, fastening the hanger firmly to the wall. Attach a carabiner to the hanger to provide a firm anchor point for your rope. Always use more than one anchor point for main belays and re-belays.

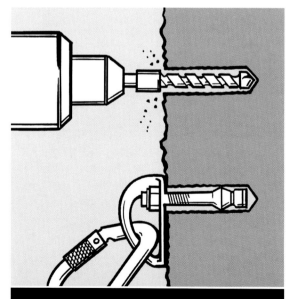

ENSURE THAT YOUR DRILL BIT HAS THE CORRECT DIAMETER SPECIFIED FOR THE BOLT AND THAT THE HOLE HAS A CLEAN EDGE.

Using SRT harnesses

SRT harnesses are not at all the same as climbing harnesses. They are designed to be safe and comfortable during the long periods you spend suspended in them, while climbing harnesses are designed to protect a climber in the event of a fall.

The SRT harness is divided into two parts. The 'sit harness' acts as your seat. It consists of a set of broad straps (around your waist and legs) joined by a D-shaped maillon, which is located in the center part. This is where all the gear attaches to the harness. When you strap in, ensure that none of the straps are twisted and that all of them are done up very tightly. Check each buckle before you begin to climb. Also ensure that the screwgate of the D-maillon faces down and that all gear is attached to its top curve, with the harness itself connected to the corners. The SRT harness is a vital part of your gear. Look after it carefully as negligence could have serious results.

n Take time to clean your harness meticulously after each use. If ingrained dirt is not carefully removed it will damage the fibers of the webbings.

n Before you commit your full weight to the harness, always check that each buckle is tight. This checking procedure should become routine and must be carried out at the top and bottom of every pitch. Buckles can work loose during ascent or descent.

n Always ensure that the buckles are double strapped.

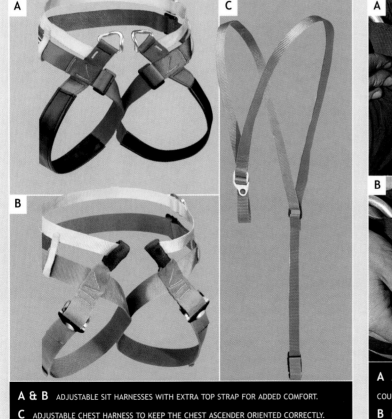

A & B ADJUSTABLE SIT HARNESSES WITH EXTRA TOP STRAP FOR ADDED COMFORT.
C ADJUSTABLE CHEST HARNESS TO KEEP THE CHEST ASCENDER ORIENTED CORRECTLY.

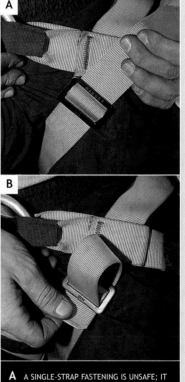

A A SINGLE-STRAP FASTENING IS UNSAFE; IT COULD SLIP OUT AND CAUSE YOU TO FALL.
B DOUBLE STRAPPING IS CORRECT.

Rigging

The art of attaching a rope to an anchor rock and guiding it to hang down freely into a pitch is known as 'rigging the pitch'. This is one of the most difficult elements of SRT and one that requires much practice. Rigging is not for beginners and should be left to experienced, qualified team members. The brief description below explains the principles of rigging.

The main belay (see below) is placed in such a way that the caver has room to attach himself safely to the main rope. Care must be taken when positioning the anchor (1): ideally, the rope must not rest on the floor or the lip of the pit, as it makes it impossible to attach a descender. Often this is unavoidable, especially near the main belay.

A backup anchor is installed to take the caver's weight if the main one fails. There must hardly be slack between them, or the caver falls the length of the slack before the backup activates. Such a fall would add strain and increase the amount of force the backup must withstand, making it much more vulnerable and less safe.

A re-belay is installed at a convenient point lower down where a deviation is impossible. The same criteria apply: anchor must be solid, rope should hang freely and there must be a backup anchor. When installing the re-belay, however, always leave about 1m (3ft) slack in the rope. It can be disadvantageous if the anchor fails, but it makes getting past the re-belay much simpler and easier, both on the way up and down. And anything that simplifies the SRT procedure usually makes it safer as well.

A rigging diagram

When rigging a pitch, the aim is to keep the rope as far as possible from the rock and any rubbing point. The rope is firmly attached at the top of the pitch using either natural anchors or bolts. The first contact point is called a top anchor or main belay (A). Use a 'Y' to distribute the load evenly. Another anchor and 'Y-front' are part way down the rope. This re-belay (B) pulls the rope away from a potential rubbing point (D). The rigger has put a further anchor (C) into the opposite wall. Instead of a re-belay the rope is simply pulled away from the rock without being firmly attached in a new place. Re-belays and deviations are installed to avoid potential rubbing points. If a rope is not long enough to reach the bottom of a pitch, two ropes are used (either joined with a knot or at a re-belay point). Note the knot at the bottom of the rope (E). This is to prevent cavers from abseiling off the end of the rope if it does not reach to the bottom of the pitch.

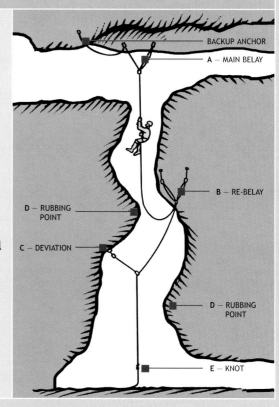

BACKUP ANCHOR
A — MAIN BELAY
B — RE-BELAY
D — RUBBING POINT
C — DEVIATION
D — RUBBING POINT
E — KNOT

Sometimes, a rope needs to be pulled away from a friction point, but a re-belay is impossible or impractical. In such cases a deviation (2) is called for. Here, too, an anchor is used (either natural feature or bolt) to attach a sling to the wall using a carabiner.

This sling is then attached to the main rope with the help of another carabiner. The sling's length determines where the rope from the other cave wall hangs.

Never attach a sling directly to a rope; always use a carabiner as link. Any friction between the two ropes could cause the main one to melt and wear through, with disastrous results.

If a deviation fails, the climber will swing away from it and pendulum across into the opposite wall.

Before any pitch can be rigged, a sturdy knot must be tied about 1.5m (5ft) from the bottom end of the rope. A firm figure 8 knot should suffice (*see* page 54).

Without such a safety knot in place, nothing would stop a caver from abseiling right off the end of the rope. This would be disastrous in cases where the rope does not reach the bottom of the pitch and could lead to serious injury.

The extra length of rope below the knot will also afford cavers enough space to attach ascenders for going up again.

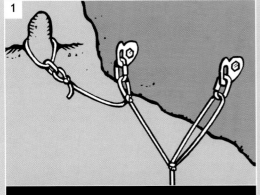

HERE A FIGURE 8 KNOT COMBINED WITH AN ALPINE BUTTERFLY IS USED TO FORM A Y-HANG FOR A MAIN ANCHOR POINT. ANOTHER FIGURE 8 OR FIGURE 9 CAN BE USED TO ATTACH IT TO A NATURAL ANCHOR AS A BACKUP.

A DEVIATION IS USED TO CHANGE THE DIRECTION OF THE ROPE WITHOUT BEING FIRMLY ATTACHED TO IT.

THE DESCENDING CAVER ABSEILING INTO THIS CAVE IS PROTECTED BY AN EXTRA ROPE CONTROLLED FROM ABOVE.

Going down

Descenders are devices that are used to abseil down a rope. Attached to the central D-maillon of the harness and to the rope, the friction created by the descender allows cavers to control the speed of their descent.

There are many different types of descenders, but cavers generally use either a rack or a bobbin device. The figure 8 device popular with climbers is not suitable for caving as it has to be detached from the caver in order to attach it to the rope. A descender is small and light so keep an extra one in your pack in case you lose or damage your main one.

Types of descenders

The popular rack descender is easy to use. It creates friction by passing the rope alternately over and under a series of bars that can slide up and down between two parallel rods. The speed of your descent is controlled by manipulating the tension in the rope below the rack, and also by applying thumb pressure on the lowest bar.

An advantage of rack descenders is that cavers can adjust the friction of the device by selecting what number of bars they wish to use. This is done during the threading process.

If you need to descend a thin rope or you have a heavy load, use more bars on the rack to increase the friction. With a light load or when abseiling down a very long rope, the weight of the rope itself may cause too much friction as you start your descent. If this happens, you will have to pull yourself down the rope to get started.

In bobbin and stop descenders the necessary friction is created by threading the rope in an S-shape over a series of pulleys and through an attached carabiner. The descent is controlled by adjusting the tension of the rope below the device.

The stop descender has a cam device attached to a handle. When the handle is released the cam automatically bites into the rope thus arresting the descent. This is a very useful safety mechanism if a falling rock

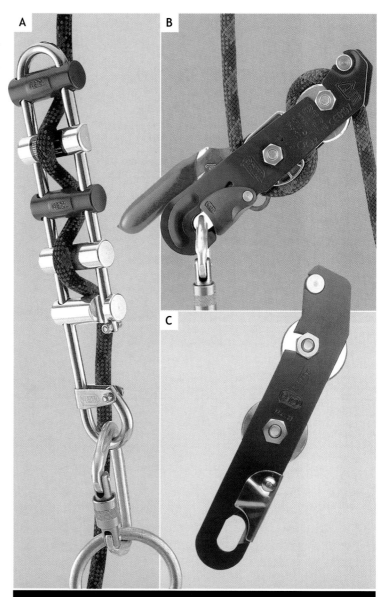

A   RACK DESCENDER: MORE BARS THREADED INCREASE FRICTION AND SLOW DESCENT.

B   STOP DESCENDER: SQUEEZE THE HANDLE TO DESCEND, RELEASE IT TO STOP.

C   BOBBIN DESCENDER: SIMILAR TO THE STOP DESCENDER, BUT WITHOUT BRAKE.

THE CAVER LEISURELY DESCENDING INTO THIS STEEP PIT IN ALABAMA, USA, IS USING A RACK TO CONTROL THE SPEED OF HIS DESCENT. WITHOUT SUCH A TOOL HE WOULD BURN HIS HANDS ON THE ROPE AND PLUMMET DOWNWARDS LIKE A ROCK.

has knocked an abseiler unconscious and temporarily disabled him. Stop devices can, however, also result in accidents. These commonly occur when the abseiler panics during a descent and instinctively grabs onto the handle, holding it tightly, thus releasing the locking mechanism on the stop device and allowing the fall to continue. Whatever type you choose, ensure that you know how it works and practice using it before you venture underground.

All descenders depend on a little slack where the rope feeds in just below the device. Without this slack there would be so much friction that the descender would not be able to move on the rope at all. The advantage of this, especially for beginners, is that a caver at the bottom of a pitch can control the descent rate of a caver who is abseiling down the rope. Thus an experienced caver can descend a pitch first and then protect a beginner as he comes down the rope after him. When caving with a novice, always ensure that an experienced caver stays behind at the top to check that the beginner gets onto the rope safely.

GOING UP A STEEPLY-RIGGED PITCH WITH THE HELP OF ASCENDERS MAY TAKE SOME TIME TO LEARN. ONCE YOU HAVE MASTERED THE SKILL, IT WILL ALLOW YOU TO EXPLORE CAVES THAT WOULD OTHERWISE BE INACCESSIBLE.

Going up

An ascender is a device that grips onto a rope when pulled in one direction, but slides freely along the rope when pulled in the other. Ascenders are generally used in pairs or threes and are attached to a caver's harness with various ropes and straps.

Although there are many ways of using ascenders, the most basic method is the so-called frog rig. In this method a caver uses two ascenders — a hand ascender attached to foot straps (the top ascender) and a chest ascender (the lower ascender). The chest ascender is attached to the D-ring of the sit harness and is kept upright by the chest harness. The upper device is attached to the D-maillon as well as the caver's feet.

To begin ascending, attach both ascender devices to the rope, moving the top device as high as possible. (The chest device will move up the rope to the height of your chest.) At this point you may have to pull the lower part of the rope down, or weigh the rope down with a tackle bag. Next, hang from the chest harness and bend your knees before moving the upper device a little higher again. Then stand up in the foot loops. These now will be slightly higher, because the hand ascender has moved up. The position of the chest ascender is raised simultaneously as you stand up. Continue repeating this process until you reach the top of the pitch.

Passing obstacles

Abseiling and prusiking (ascending a rope) are simple and uncomplicated procedures if the rope hangs freely down the middle of a chamber. When deviations and re-belays have been installed for additional support, they become trickier and as you descend or ascend, re-belays can become obstacles.

Ensure that your instructor teaches you how to pass obstacles when approaching from above and below. You will also have to learn how to change direction while you are on the rope. These advanced techniques are very important and must be thoroughly practiced under the tuition of an experienced SRT instructor until you have mastered them and feel confident enough to use them in a cave.

FROG RIG: **A** BODY WEIGHT IS TAKEN BY THE CHEST ASCENDER; HAND ASCENDER RAISES FOOT LOOPS. **B** HAND ASCENDER BEARS THE LOAD AS CAVER STANDS IN FOOT LOOPS AND RAISES CHEST ASCENDER.

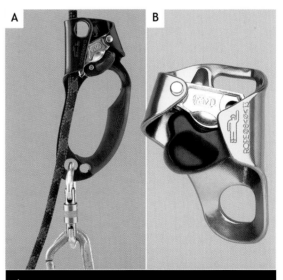

A THE HAND ASCENDER IS ATTACHED TO THE FOOT LOOPS. THE CAM BITES INTO THE ROPE TO PREVENT IT FROM SLIPPING.
B A CHEST ASCENDER OR CROLL IS ATTACHED BETWEEN THE D-MAILLON ON THE SEAT HARNESS AND THE CHEST HARNESS.

Going Caving

Caving is a potentially dangerous activity so no outing should be taken lightly. Never underestimate your chances of getting hurt or meeting some other ill fate. Good preparation and thorough planning are essential — the success or failure of a caving trip is often determined long before you get to the cave. As a newcomer to the sport you will not be required to do much planning until you have gained more experience. However, some basic rules and considerations must always be known and adhered to by all — even novices.

Permission

Many caves are no longer accessible to cavers because previous teams failed to get the necessary permission.

Very few cavers are fortunate enough to have free access to land on which caves are found. Before you set off on any expedition, obtain permission from the relevant authority. If you need to travel across privately owned land in order to reach the cave, be sure to approach the legal owner of the property in advance. Access procedures are often published in guide books or available from local caving organizations.

Contingency planning

Caving accidents can happen unexpectedly so it is vital to take certain precautions beforehand just in case things go wrong. The leader of the expedition should leave important details about the route and the caving team with a responsible contact person, who should also receive detailed instructions about what to do in case of an emergency. If possible, the contact person should be an experienced caver too, preferably even someone who knows the cave you intend to visit so that he or she is able to judge whether something has gone wrong or not. The family of each team member must know who this anchor person is and be able to contact him or her if they have any concerns.

The team and its leader

Before you go on a caving trip you should know why you want to visit that particular cave — be it to conduct a survey or purely for the adventure of caving as a sport.

The team should always match the objectives of the trip and vice versa. This means that the type of cave and the reason for your visit will determine the team members, their level of experience and expertise.

The contact sheet

Remember to provide the most important details to your contact person before every trip. These should be presented in the form of a contact sheet and include (not necessarily in this order): the full name of the team leader; the name of the cave; date of departure; date and estimated time of return; the name of the cave entrance; intended route through the cave (if applicable); the team's details (names and surnames); everyone's personal contact numbers; the relevant emergency or rescue organizations and their correct telephone numbers. Also important are:
■ Location of the cave, as well as your method of transport, vehicle's registration details and your intended itinerary (if you need to travel some distance to get there).
■ Your expected return time should always include a reasonable leeway period (calculated in hours) to allow for unforeseen delays, before your designated contact person calls for help.

opposite IF YOU HAPPEN UPON AN INTERESTING CAVE OPENING ON YOUR OWN, NEVER ATTEMPT TO ENTER AND EXPLORE SINGLE-HANDEDLY EVEN THOUGH YOU MAY BE SORELY TEMPTED — CAVING IS NOT A SOLITARY SPORT. ARRANGE AN OUTING AND RETURN WITH A TEAM.

Although some experienced teams, especially those who often go caving together, can do without a formal leader, most groups will appoint one person to take responsibility for the safety of the entire team.

A leader will have to think and act in the interest of all participants, and must have the courage to make judgement calls when required to do so. His or her duty begins with a careful evaluation of the intended caving outing and its specific degree of difficulty versus the levels of experience present in the team. If technical rope work is required, for instance, the entire team must be suitably qualified to go on the trip.

Not everyone is cut out to lead — certain qualities make some people better leaders than others:

■ A leader is responsible for the team and must assess the ability and experience of each member to ensure that everyone is suitably qualified for the trip. Emergency procedures and thorough contingency plans are put in place by the leader.

You — the team member

Before you join a caving outing, you must know your own abilities and make sure that the leader, too, is aware of your limitations, lack of skill or experience. You should also inform your team leader of any medical conditions you suffer from. Have realistic expectations of what the trip will entail and you will not be disappointed.

■ Confidence and experience are required to lead a team into a cave and safely back out again.

■ The team leader needs to ensure that all team members know exactly what to expect from the trip and what special gear they should bring along.

In teams that include one or more beginners (or a caver who is seriously out of practice), the leader's role becomes even more important, since inexperience or

TRAINING TRIPS INTO SIMPLE HORIZONTAL CAVE STRUCTURES AFFORD BEGINNERS AN EXCELLENT OPPORTUNITY TO LEARN FROM THEIR MORE EXPERIENCED TEAMMATES, BECAUSE THE ELEMENT OF DANGER IS KEPT TO AN ABSOLUTE MINIMUM.

TEAM SPIRIT, CAMARADERIE AND MUTUAL RESPECT ARE THE INGREDIENTS THAT ENSURE A PLEASANT OUTING. THE LEADER'S CHALLENGING ROLE AS GUIDE, MOTIVATOR AND DECISION MAKER IS MADE MUCH EASIER IF THE OTHERS RESPECT HIS OR HER AUTHORITY.

ignorance cannot be allowed to endanger an entire team. The leader must sometimes overrule a decision made by someone else and have the courage to do so. Although this may not earn popularity points, it will be in the team's best interest and, therefore, to everyone's benefit.

As the team leader will be responsible for the safety of the whole team, the choice should always fall on an experienced caver who is able to calmly guide and advise beginners in an unfamiliar environment.

If you are planning a working trip, such as a cave survey or a photographic session, for example, it is best to keep the team as small as possible. Working teams tend to move through a cave very slowly because each member has a specific task to perform. Since not many people are required to do what needs to be done, the others could end up sitting around bored and cold.

For training trips into easy caves, ensure that there is a good mix of experienced and novice cavers (the exact proportion will depend on the cave) so that the beginners have an opportunity to learn. Technical training trips into vertical caves require a much higher proportion of experienced cavers than sightseeing trips into horizontal caverns.

Getting there

Getting to a cave can be just as exciting and dangerous as getting into it. Many good caving areas are densely populated and it is often possible to drive right up to the entrance of a cave. However, if you intend caving in a remote wilderness, ensure that there is someone with you who knows the access route.

You may need to hire a local guide, so send out a reconnaissance team before the main team starts out. You should also have a detailed topographical map of the area (one that shows specific landmarks and physical features such as rivers and mountains) to avoid getting lost.

A COMPASS, MAP AND GPS DEVICE WILL HELP YOU FIND YOUR WAY TO A REMOTE CAVE AND, MORE IMPORTANTLY, BACK HOME AGAIN.

Away from the main roads, reliable maps and a Global Positioning System (GPS) receiver — available from any good outdoor supplier — will make navigation easier. A GPS device uses satellites to determine your position, anywhere in the world, to within 10m (33ft); depending on location and number of satellites it can detect, it may even be 10 times as accurate. (Note: although a GPS receiver can determine latitude and longitude, it is ineffective for determining altitude.)

Before you drive your vehicle to a cave, check that the access area is not in restricted territory and be sure to obtain permits and permissions. If you have to cross private property, show consideration by leaving land and gates the way you found them. A friendly land owner will not be quite as accommodating next time, if his prize bull escapes through a gate you left open.

Pre-trip briefing

Before starting out on an expedition, the leader should brief the team to ensure that they have realistic expectations and know what is expected of them.

During this briefing the leader must discuss aspects such as the walk into the cave, he must also highlight the potential dangers, mention specific requirements of the trip, point out obstacles that may be encountered and state any other relevant information about the environment the team is about to enter. The briefing is also an opportunity to put novices at ease by answering any questions they may have.

All team members must be informed of the expected duration of the trip. In addition, the briefing should inform everyone about emergency procedures and any contingency plans that have been put in place in the event of an accident. It is essential that each member knows exactly what to do in an emergency.

Some caves contain sensitive areas to which entry is prohibited for safety or conservation reasons, or due to ongoing scientific research. While obtaining permission to visit a cave, i.e. during the planning stages in preparation for the outing, a team leader would have enquired with the relevant authorities whether any such limitations apply to the cave or the territory in which it is located. If restrictions do apply, these are shared with the team in the briefing session (and if it is a cave your team has visited before, this is an excellent time to remind them of no-go areas).

Flagging tape (similar to the plastic tape the police use to cordon off sensitive areas) is sometimes used underground to restrict access or demarcate clear routes through vulnerable areas. Note that this tape is used to mark the path you should tread on, and in rare instances to block off entire areas no one should venture into. All the cavers in your group must know exactly what the tape means, where they can expect to find it and how they should proceed.

If you use a survey map to assist navigation through the cave, team members should familiarize themselves with the survey and the intended route. This will give newcomers to the cave an idea of what to expect and lessen their chances of getting lost.

ENERGY RICH SNACKS SUCH AS GRANOLA- OR YOGURT BARS AND DEXTROSE TABLETS DON'T TAKE UP MUCH SPACE AND CAN BE CARRIED ALONG IN YOUR PACK. EAT A HEALTHY BREAKFAST BEFORE YOUR TRIP, BUT IF YOU DO GET HUNGRY IN THE CAVE A CANDY OR CHOCOLATE BAR WILL PROVIDE THE BODY WITH AN INSTANTLY ACCESSIBLE SOURCE OF ENERGY IN THE FORM OF REFINED SUGAR THAT WILL BOOST YOUR STAMINA.

Food for energy

Caving requires an enormous amount of energy, so it is important to ensure that you have enough sustenance and good general fitness that will allow you to complete the caving trip. Consult a dietician for advice if you have any concerns or need to establish whether your food intake is balanced. If you are able to partake in a strenuous day-long mountain walk, you should be fit enough to go caving for a day.

Your muscles and brain utilize glucose as their main source of energy. Although muscles can also use fats as a fuel, they will burn sugar first, so aim to keep the glucose levels in your blood relatively constant. Two main sources of glucose are readily available: sweet foods that contain refined sugar (i.e. chocolate bars) and in carbohydrate-rich foods such as apples, pears, lentils, beans and oats. Before you go on a strenuous caving trip boost your system by consuming complex carbohydrates the night before, just as any other sportsman or woman would, to ensure a relatively slow release of energy throughout the next day (the body converts carbohydrates into glucose).

Begin the day you go caving with a good breakfast of oat porridge to boost your carbohydrate levels. If you really must have eggs and bacon, add a good helping of baked beans to provide the necessary slow release of energy you will need. If you are going caving for the entire day take along oatmeal crunchies or granola snack bars. Even a light sandwich will boost blood sugar levels significantly, but be sure to store your sandwiches in a tightly sealed plastic container, or they will degenerate into an unappetizing soggy lump at the bottom of your bag.

If you require an energy boost in the cave, candy bars are good for this as they provide your body with energy in a ready-to-use form. Keep a few small chocolate bars handy, to use as energy top-ups before a long climb or a very tight squeeze through a narrow passage. They will also be useful in cold conditions, because the instant fuel is burned by the body quickly to keep you warm. If you are feeling light-headed, your blood sugar levels may be low: sit down, rest for a while and suck a glucose sweet.

Sufficient water intake is a must on caving trips, as the body can dehydrate alarmingly quickly. Plan on drinking at least one liter of water per day while you are underground — even more if you are in a hot cave. It is advisable to take potable water into the cave with you rather than run the risk of having to drink polluted or contaminated water underground.

WATER ALWAYS PRESENTS A DANGER IN FLOODED CAVES, EVEN IF IT DOES NOT GUSH AS STRONGLY AS IN CUEVA DEL AGUA, SPAIN.

Equipment

The type of cave and the planned route will determine the equipment you take along. After consulting with the leader, select the appropriate gear. It is a good idea to take a little extra in case of an emergency, but the key is to pack wisely. Too much equipment will weigh you down, slow your progress and make your caving trip a miserable haul. (*See* Chapter 3.)

Hidden hazards

Although the dark underground environment can be dangerous, you can avoid most caving hazards quite simply by possessing adequate knowledge about them. Apart from the obvious perils presented by tripping, falling into pits, banging your head and being hit by falling rocks, you will need to know how to cope with several other situations.

Flooding

When you begin planning a trip, find out from the land owner or your local caving club whether the cave you intend visiting is prone to floods.

If there is any risk of flooding, take the warning seriously. Before venturing into the cave, contact the local weather station and also ask the opinion of local cavers who know the area. If wet weather has been predicted, postpone your trip.

Cave diseases

Any waterborne diseases occurring in the surface water of a particular area is likely to be present underground as well, so cavers should be aware of them.

Again, check with local caving clubs and the health authorities before you go, or you could land up drinking what may look and taste clean, but contains parasites like roundworm, bilharzia or giardiasis. If you have to drink cave water, take preventive measures by using water-purifying tablets. Obtainable at most outdoor shops, these tablets are inexpensive and easy to use, but ensure that you follow the instructions carefully.

Histoplasmosis is a fungus that grows on bat guano and bird droppings. Although it often occurs in caves that house bat colonies, it is more common in warmer,

Flood warning signs

■ Once you are inside a cave, look on the walls as you go along. Horizontal lines of small sticks, organic matter and stains often indicate the high-tide mark of a previous flood.

■ Take note of chambers located above this line — they can be used as a safe haven in the case of a flash-flood emergency.

■ Keep a check on the level of streams in the cave by comparing the water level to a fixed object such as a protruding rock.

■ Another way to detect an increase in water flow is to watch the water dripping from cave decorations. When the drip from a stalagtite changes to a steady trickle, chances are good that it has begun to rain outside.

■ If you do get caught in a flooded cave, look for a spot that is sufficiently high and dry and wait. Do not attempt to fight your way out through a raging torrent of water.

■ If you are still dry, aim to stay that way. You may have to wait for a long time before water levels drop and must conserve your body heat.

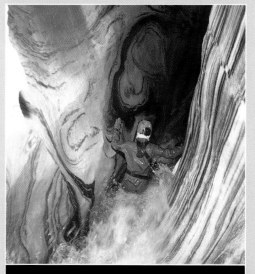

BE WARY OF RUSHING STREAMS. THEY MAY LOOK MEEK YET THE CURRENT MAY BE POWERFUL ENOUGH TO SWEEP YOU AWAY.

drier caves. Exposure causes flu-like symptoms, as well as coughing and a headache, but can be quite serious. If you feel as though you are suffering from flu about a week after visiting a guano cave, tell your doctor where you have been as it may help him with the diagnosis.

Avoid caves that are known to be infected, or wear a face mask that filters the air you breathe. Check with health authorities for suitable specifications.

Caving accidents

If your team has met with misfortune in a cave, either in the form of an accident or by getting lost in an unfamiliar system of passages, a number of crucial decisions will have to be made. The most important of these is whether to stay where you are and wait until help arrives, or try and find your way back to the cave entrance and the outside world.

Getting lost

Losing your way can be a serious problem, especially in larger cave systems. If you are unfamiliar with the cave you are going to explore, it is essential that you try beforehand to obtain a survey map from a local caving club to assist you. Remember to keep a constant check on your position while you venture in deeper.

Some clubs publish their own guides to popular caves in the area and also provide surveys and useful practical information regarding any special equipment that may be required, as well as possible hazards.

If no survey is available, you will have to memorize your route. This takes practice as cave passages tend to look very different on the way out. A good tip is to turn around every now and again while you are going into the cave, to see what the passage looks like when you are facing the other way.

Build a small cairn (pile of stones) at the exit of a passage when you enter a larger chamber. There may be other passages that look very similar to the one you came from and you could get lost in a maze. The cairn serves as an indicator for the correct exit passage.

If you are completely lost, rely on the contingency plans you have made. Keep your group together, stay where you are and wait for help to arrive. You are expected back at a certain time and someone will come looking for you if you don't show up. There is nothing to do but wait, save battery power and try and remain warm by sitting huddled together. If you have made no contingency plans, or been unable to do so — do not chance getting lost! Don't venture into unknown systems and don't explore too deeply.

While you wait for rescue

■ Keep the team together at all costs. Do not be tempted to split the group by sending a search party to look for possible exit routes. This could delay the rescuers, who would then have to look for the missing few who are wandering around in other parts of the cave.

■ Focus on keeping warm. You'll feel cold quickly once you stop moving around. Climb into your survival bag if you have one to reduce the loss of body heat. If you have a carbide lamp, the gas generator gives off much heat. Keep it inside your bag to warm yourself. If you do not have a carbide lamp, keep a lit candle inside the bag, but watch the flame; don't set yourself on fire.

■ Prevent hypothermia by keeping off the cave floor. Rather sit on your caving bag, a coiled up rope or other suitable item that can provide some insulation, and huddle together for warmth.

■ Conserve light by switching all of them off. If you need a light for comfort or to boost group morale, use one at a time. A candle is a good light source while you wait for rescue.

■ Conserve water and food items. If an extended waiting period seems likely and the cave is dry, use your drinking water sparingly. Your body should have enough energy stored to last a long time before you need to eat again, but a little chocolate may boost morale.

IN THE EVENT OF A SERIOUS ACCIDENT, STABILIZE AND IMMOBILIZE THE
PATIENT BEFORE MOVING HIM OR HER, OR WAIT UNTIL HELP ARRIVES.

Coping with injuries

Although detailed first-aid information is not within
the scope of this book, every caver should know some
general rules and have an idea of how to cope with
injuries. If you intend to go caving on a regular basis,
join one of the hands-on first-aid courses offered by a
reputable training organization. The first step with an
injured patient is to assess the situation:

HAZARDS: Check that the hazard which caused the
injury is no longer a factor. If a caver was hit by a
falling rock, check that rescuers can safely go in to
assist or you may end up with more than one patient.

HELLO: Check to see that the patient is conscious. A
caver who is awake may be able to tell you where the
pain is and whether movement is possible.

If the patient is unconscious, do not move him.
Always treat unconscious patients as if they have
sustained a neck injury. Restrict movement of the neck
and spine to an absolute minimum until the patient has
been stabilized by a medical rescue team.

HELP: Once the hazard has been removed from the
patient, or vice versa, keep the patient warm and send
for help. Moving an injured teammate through a cave
is very difficult and may further endanger him, so call
for professional medical help right away.

Watch out for hypothermia

Hypothermia is a potentially life-threatening condition
that sets in when the body rapidly loses so much heat
that its internal temperature sinks below a level at
which life can be sustained. This is a surreptitious and
particularly dangerous threat to cavers because it is
associated with cold, wet or windy conditions and the
onset of the symptoms is insidious.

It is essential for every caver to be able to recognize
the warning signs of early-stage hypothermia and know
how to combat the condition quickly and effectively.
Unless further heat loss is prevented, a patient's condition will deteriorate rapidly, eventually resulting in
coma, cardiac arrest and death. Immediate treatment
for hypothermia victims entails stopping to rest where
you are and warming the patient without delay. The
early warning signs are:

■ Uncontrollable fits of shivering and a very intense
feeling of cold.

■ Confusion, poor judgement and irritability.

■ Repeated stumbling, slurred speech.

■ Stiff muscles.

■ Cold, blue feet and hands.

The ABC principle

If a caver is unconscious, use the internationally
accepted ABC first-aid principle:

A — AIRWAY: check that nothing is blocking the
patient's airway. Noisy breathing often indicates
a problem. Remove any obstruction with your
fingers if possible.

B — BREATHING: check that the patient's chest
is rising and falling. If it is not, attempt mouth-
to-mouth resuscitation. Try not to twist the
patient's neck as it could be broken.

C — CIRCULATION: check the major artery in
the neck or groin to see if there is a pulse. If
not, begin cardiopulmonary resuscitation (CPR)
on the patient immediately.

Emergency kits

There are a few articles that should form part of every caver's pack, whether he is going on a short adventure outing or a lengthy surveying expedition. It is always advisable to be prepared rather than suffer the consequences of negligence. In addition to personal kits, the group should also carry a solid-fuel stove and fuel tablets with which to heat water — to be used for a warm drink underground or to raise a caver's body temperature before hypothermia sets in. Outdoor outfitters offer convenient containers, sometimes already stocked with an assortment of useful items, so there is really no excuse for not having one. If you prefer to organize your own kit, here are a few articles you may wish to include, although the list is by no means comprehensive.

■ DUCT TAPE is extremely versatile, as it can hold almost anything together, from wet suits to open wounds. If you do not want to carry along a full roll, keep a few strips of it wrapped around your helmet.

■ A SURVIVAL BAG, made of thin plastic and thus conveniently lightweight, is big enough to accommodate an adult body. It slows down the loss of heat by keeping a layer of air trapped around the body and is very useful in cold caves to prevent hypothermia. It takes up very little space and will keep you warm if you have to sit for an extended period.

■ A WATERPROOF TORCH need not have the same power as your main caving beam, but should have a long battery life. The small LED-based variety is ideal as it can provide over 100 hours of light.

■ BANDAGE AND STERILE DRESSING, if not too bulky, can be slipped into your helmet. Remember, however, that the air space in your helmet is there for your protection, so do not use it as an all-purpose storage space.

■ CANDLES, MATCHES AND A LIGHTER will not only supply you with comforting light in the event of a long wait, but can also help to keep you warm. Conventional matches do not normally last long underground, especially when the box gets wet, and waterproof matches are not always reliable. A cigarette lighter in a sealed plastic bag is a much better idea.

■ A GOOD PENKNIFE should be reasonably compact even though it is fitted with a variety of tools that are useful in many situations. A good alternative is a rescue knife, similar in size to a penknife but with a folding blade that locks into position when open. The advantage of this knife is that it can be opened with one hand, useful if you need to cut something while abseiling down a rope and only have one hand to spare.

■ FOOD such as a few granola bars and slabs of chocolate will keep you going in emergencies. Depending on your personal preference you could also take nuts, dried fruit and glucose sweets.

Post trip

When all the members of your team have successfully completed their caving adventure and returned to the surface, the trip is far from over. A number of things remain to be done.

■ Let your surface contact person know that you have returned safely. This will prevent a rescue team from being called out unnecessarily.

■ Hold a detailed debrief session. This is a valuable learning tool for novices and can also benefit the more experienced caver. If there were incidents or accidents underground, talk about what went wrong and why, and discuss possible preventive measures that could become useful for future trips.

■ If the purpose of your outing trip was for anything other than just sport, write a detailed trip report. This is particularly important if any scientific work was done. While these reports can simply be kept for future reference, they are far more valuable when they are shared with other cavers by publishing them in a club newsletter or journal. Big and well-manned expeditions often result in an entire book being published afterwards.

■ In order to maintain cordial relations with landowners, the very least you should do is thank them for allowing you on their property. This will facilitate access to the cave the next time, whether it is for your own benefit or that of other cavers. If you write a trip report, send a courtesy copy to the landowners — they like to know what is happening on their land.

Sensible caving

Every caver must have at least a basic knowledge of how to get out of a nasty situation, or assist a teammate who is in trouble or injured. This is particularly important when you have gone on a caving expedition in a remote area that does not have the infrastructure to support an organized mountain or caving rescue team.

Your foremost aim should be not to endanger yourself or others in the first place. If you use your common sense and adhere to a few simple rules,

the outing is sure to be a fun-filled and interesting adventure, rather than a harrowing experience.

■ Memorize your route through the cave and take whatever precaution you can to avoid getting lost.

■ At least one member of your team must have a working knowledge of first-aid routines and should carry a small medical kit.

■ Especially important for vertical caves is that you should always carry spare equipment with you, in case your primary equipment fails or is lost down a steep crack and cannot be retrieved.

■ Learn how to use alternative methods for climbing and descending ropes. It is good to know how to use prusik knots instead of ascenders, or rappel (abseil) without a descender. Although these techniques are more dangerous than actually using the correct equipment, they could be a lifesaver one day, so ask your SRT instructor to teach them to you.

COLD, HUNGRY AND VERY MUDDY, A SPELEOLOGIST RETURNS FROM A SUCCESSFUL CAVING TRIP TIRED AND WORN-OUT, BUT SATISFIED WITH THE ADVENTURE HE HAS HAD IN THE MYSTERIOUS SUBTERRANEAN ENVIRONMENT.

Special
Interest

Caves and caving offer such a wide range of activities that specialization in a particular area is almost inevitable. A major field of interest is cave diving, where experienced scuba divers do their exploration underwater to probe the courses of water-filled cave passages. This is such a highly specialized activity, however, that it cannot be covered in a beginner's guide. Here are two other and far less extreme activities that beginners are bound to come across: survey and photography.

Surveying a cave

Explorers make their mark by recording what they do and where they go. Cave explorers are no exception and many invest enormous amounts of time and effort in producing maps (surveys) of the caves they explore.

Basic surveying principles

When you begin a survey, keep in mind your reasons for doing so as this will influence the way in which you go about collecting data, as well as the type of information you gather and its accuracy.

If the final survey drawing is to be used as a general map for cave navigation, then the survey team must record information that will enable the end user to glean information about the cave's layout and so decide what special equipment he may need to bring along. A geologist doing a cave survey, on the other hand, would be much more interested in the strata, rock type and passage cross sections, as well as the physical detail found on the cave walls, while a zoologist would want to find out in which part of the cave bats or cave insects occur and why.

The method for gathering data has not changed for years. Surveyors move systematically through the cave using a compass, clinometer (*see* page 76) and tape measure to record their progress. They do this by fixing points along their route, which are known as stations.

The instruments are then used to take accurate measurements from one beacon to the next until the entire cave has been traversed. Once all the measurements are in, they are fed into a special computer program that changes the raw instrument readings into a continuous line which represents the path the surveyors have taken through the cave.

As the survey team moves along, they take note of the passage walls — one member of the team records a scale drawing — as well as their exact location in relation to the survey stations. (Apart from cave walls, illustrators frequently also record characteristic features.) The drawings are later superimposed on the plotted coordinates of the stations to create an overview of the survey. This gives an indication of the physical nature and extent of the cave.

Survey stations

When taking an instrument reading, get someone to place a torch on the far beacon so that you can sight on it. Small beacons using LEDs can be useful as they provide enough light to take a reading and will often run on batteries that are too flat for any other use.

When you get to an important point such as an intersection, or to the end of a surveying session, you may need to make a permanent mark. A good tip is to describe the beacon and its location in great detail in your survey notes.

The type of permanent beacon marker you choose will depend on the type of cave in which the survey is being done. A piece of flagging tape under a rock will remain in a dry cave for many years, but would not survive that next rainstorm in a flood-prone area.

opposite CAVE SURVEYS WILL ALLOW YOU TO EXPLORE AND MAP THE CAPTIVATING SUBTERRANEAN WORLDS. THIS SURVEYOR USES A NON-MAGNETIC LAMP TO LIGHT A SIGHTING COMPASS DURING A SURVEY.

Survey instruments

Although several different types of survey instruments are available from specialist sources, compasses and clinometers are still the most popular choice among cavers. These instruments comprise a small plastic module that is housed in an aluminum body. This makes them more durable and able to withstand the odd fall to the cave floor. Some models have built-in lights, while others rely on external sources.

Surveying with a compass, clinometer and tape can, however, lead to certain inaccuracies, especially when large cave systems are surveyed. The teams usually reach a joint decision as to whether they accept their first attempt as accurate enough or go back in and resurvey the inaccurate parts. One way to improve the accuracy of a survey is to use instruments that are more precise and capable of exact readings.

The theodolite and laser range finder commonly used by surface surveyors may give better results under good conditions, but caves seldom provide floors that are flat enough or passages that are sufficiently high to allow the use of such cumbersome instruments. Apart from physical limitations, not many cavers can afford such expensive equipment.

The survey book

The survey book is used to record all measurements and drawings. Some surveyors prefer a bound book that keeps all the data neatly together, while others opt for

A SURVEY RECORDER NOTES ALL INSTRUMENT READINGS AND COMPLETE SCALED SKETCHES OF THE CAVE PLAN, PROFILE AND CROSS SECTIONS.

How to read a compass and clinometer

- To take a compass reading, line the sighting line in the compass up with an imaginary line running from the nearest beacon to the next.
- Ensure that the compass disc is level and that it can rotate freely.
- Ensure that the sighting line in the compass is midway between the vertical blanks found in the eyepiece.
- Once the compass disc has stopped turning, read the bearing through the eyepiece. If you have to shine light onto the compass to improve visibility, ensure that you use a non-magnetic light source. Anything that is magnetic (such as a hand torch and some helmet fittings) may cause errors in the reading.
- If you must use a hand torch, carry out tests first to determine a safe distance between the torch and the compass so that readings will not be affected. Also check that your helmet does not affect the accuracy of the compass reading.

loose leaves of waterproof paper that can be kept in an aluminum cover as additional protection.

The data-gathering section of a survey book is usually laid out in columns under the following headings with a measurement taken for each one: *From beacon*; *To beacon*; *Compass*; *Clinometer*; *Tape*; *Left wall*; *Right wall*; *Ceiling*; *Floor*; *Comment*.

To reduce blunders it is good practice to take each reading more than once. Surveyors often take backsights. This means that they will take a reading from Beacon A to Beacon B, then measure the same leg again, but this time from Beacon B to Beacon A. The compass readings should be exactly 180 degrees from each other, and the clinometer readings should be identical, but with the sign reversed. If you have the choice, always get a compass that does not have forward and reverse readings on the same scale. It is far too easy to read the wrong scale by mistake.

Survey terms

In order to grasp how a team of surveyors determines the look and extent of a cave or cave system, it is necessary to understand the visual tools they have at their disposal to record what they see. Below is a brief explanation of the ones that are most commonly used.

A The plan of a cave is very similar to the blueprint of a house. It represents a bird's-eye-view onto a horizontal cutaway. Plans are excellent for depicting the layout of simple caves that are mostly horizontal and on one level only. They fail when they need to reveal information about vertical areas of caves and can become confusing when a cave has several horizontal layers stacked one above the other.

B The profile is what you would see if you could make a vertical cut through a cave and then look at it from the side. The angle at which the imaginary slice is taken is carefully determined so that the resulting profile gives the most meaningful and represent-ative picture of the cave (usually along a section of passage that clearly shows variations in floor and ceiling height).

C The simple cross section is a slice of the cave taken across a cave passage, and is usually drawn to give an indication of the shape of the passage. Cross sections often highlight how a cave was formed, as different types of formation processes result in characteristic passage cross sections.

D The 3-D cross section is a detailed representation of the cave and the geological area that surrounds it. By slicing away two imaginary sections, the layout of the cave and the reason for its formation become much clearer.

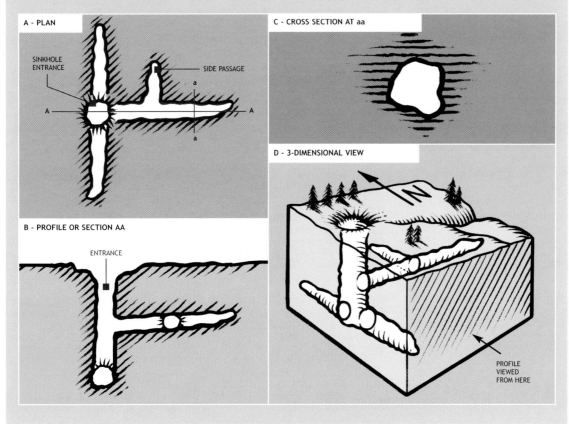

A - PLAN

SINKHOLE ENTRANCE

SIDE PASSAGE

C - CROSS SECTION AT aa

D - 3-DIMENSIONAL VIEW

B - PROFILE OR SECTION AA

ENTRANCE

PROFILE VIEWED FROM HERE

Survey symbols

To make cave surveys readable for cavers everywhere no matter what language they speak, the member countries of the *Union Internationale de Spéléologie* (UIS) agreed on a standard list of symbols that are now used on all survey maps worldwide. These are just a handful of the many symbols cave surveyors use. Visit the UIS website (*see* page 93) for the complete set.

Obstruction in a passage due to a change in height (more than 1m; 3ft) is indicated with a plus or minus sign.

For slopes greater than 45° (arrow heads point down the slope that is to be indicated).

Denotes a section obstructed by large boulders (best route through the obstruction is indicated by thicker line).

Dotted outline of cave areas whose dimensions were not properly measured.

Indicates a change of survey grade, or any other limit that must be show.

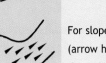

Location of a cross section with indication of reference number and direction of view.

Position of a permanently marked survey station (not shown if the symbol would obscure other map detail).

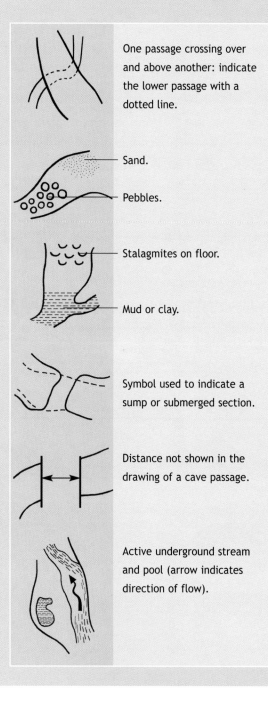

One passage crossing over and above another: indicate the lower passage with a dotted line.

Sand.

Pebbles.

Stalagmites on floor.

Mud or clay.

Symbol used to indicate a sump or submerged section.

Distance not shown in the drawing of a cave passage.

Active underground stream and pool (arrow indicates direction of flow).

Cave photography

Caves provide some of the most spectacular natural beauty and are ideal subjects for photographers. Since most of the potential images are hidden in darkness, aspirant cave photographers have to overcome unusual obstacles and learn a very specialized form of photography that is technically very challenging.

Cameras

Before you invest in high-tech equipment and rush off, speak to an experienced cave photographer or consult your local photography club or a camera shop for sound advice. Almost any type of camera can be used in cave photography, provided that it has a few basic features, the most important of which is the ability to trigger a flash. Most compact cameras come with a built-in flash and do not have the capacity to trigger an external one manually. This drawback can be overcome by using a separate, or 'slave', flash unit that can extend the power of even the smallest autofocus camera. Digital cameras are increasingly popular. The better quality ones have numerous settings, are totally controllable and can also be used with separate dedicated flashguns.

Most cave photographers still opt for a 35mm SLR camera, because this type of equipment offers a reasonable trade-off between its built-in features, relatively light weight and good picture quality.

Although SLRs have a clear advantage when it comes to choosing additional lenses, some autofocus models have so many attractive features that they have become an attractive alternative to the bigger and heavier SLR versions.

Ultimately, your choice will depend on your needs and your pocket, as well as the type of photography that interests you. If you just want to fill an album with attractive keepsakes of your caving adventures, a simple compact camera will suffice.

If you intend to sell your images commercially, however, you will require much more sophisticated and expensive equipment to ensure that your photographs are of a sufficiently high standard and quality.

Certain camera settings are essential if you wish to make use of the open-shutter techniques. 'B' and 'T' settings allow a photographer to keep the shutter open while firing a series of flashes in different directions and over a relatively long period of time. This enables the photographer to light up different parts of the cave using only one flash. (The 'B' setting keeps the shutter open as long as the shutter button is depressed, while the 'T' setting opens the shutter on the first press and closes it on the second.)

When it comes to choosing camera lenses, a general rule is: the wider the lens, the better the picture. This holds true in most cases, even for a telephoto lens — especially in small cave passages. Here, it avoids the

WHILE THE PHOTOGRAPHER FOCUSES ON THE IMAGE, THE PATIENT HELPER HOLDS ALOFT THE SLAVE FLASH READY TO FIRE WHEN HE IS PROMPTED TO DO SO.

effect of standing in a tunnel during the taking of the picture. Long, or zoom, lenses are useful when you want to take a picture of delicate cave formations or animals that are further away (such as bats roosting on the ceiling of a chamber or a high passage). It is very easy to get too close to a small formation and break it off while you're trying to photograph it. A zoom enables you to take the picture from far away.

Tripod

If you wish to employ the open-shutter technique, a tripod is essential. The camera must not move a fraction during the time that the shutter is fully open or your picture will be a blurred disappointment. A cable release is a must-have for the same reason. The press of a finger on the camera shutter release could make even the sturdiest tripod wobble slightly, resulting in another ruined image.

Remember that your tripod will have to withstand many trips underground and may often be planted in mud, so choose a sturdy model that can be cleaned easily (tripods with U-channel legs are easier to clean than those featuring tubular legs).

THE GOLONDRINAS PIT IN MEXICO IS SPECTACULARLY LIT WITH POWERFUL LIGHTS POSITIONED AT SEVERAL STRATEGIC POINTS TO PRODUCE THIS BREATHTAKING ENVIRONMENT.

Lighting

The permanent darkness of a cave environment means that the photographer will have to provide all the lighting he requires. Although having to haul cumbersome lighting systems just to take a few pictures may sound like a disadvantage, it does provide an opportunity for some interesting techniques that can produce spectacularly striking results.

Electronic flashes produce highly directional harsh light. When mounted close to the lens, they tend to 'flatten' the subject. Always aim to move the flash some distance away from the camera to counteract this effect; even a short distance can make a remarkable difference. An electronic flash produces a very short burst of light that lasts no more than a few thousandths of a second. This is helpful when you are trying to 'freeze' action in an image.

If you want to take a picture of an underground waterfall, on the other hand, an electronic flash would not be the best choice of lighting as it would freeze the action of the falling stream, making it resemble a series of water bubbles caught in mid-air. There are two ways of getting around this problem. Extend the duration of your flash by having it flash a few times in quick succession, or use several flashes attached to a special device that allows you to trigger them — one after the other — in a rapid sequence.

Alternatively, you could also use a light with a longer duration, such as is provided by a flash bulb or tungsten light. Flash bulbs, sadly, are difficult to obtain nowadays, as they are no longer produced and not commercially available anymore. Seasoned cave photographers love them, however, because they burn magnesium contained in the bulb to produce a much stronger, brighter and lasting flash than that emitted by an electronic model, and disperse their light evenly in all directions.

Tungsten lighting can also be used for cave photography, but it may be difficult to control the color balance and brightness it offers.

The first challenge is transporting a tungsten light that is powerful enough to light a chamber down into the cave. When that is resolved, you have to overcome a color-balance problem, because tungsten light is very yellow when compared to the other flash-lights that are available on the market. To avoid a yellowish tinge in your cave pictures, you need to buy a film that is matched to the light that you are going to use.

THE OPEN-SHUTTER HAS CAPTURED THE BEAM OF THE BRIGHT HEADLAMP WHILE AN ELECTRONIC FLASH HAS FROZEN THE MOVEMENT OF THE CAVER.

Some useful photographic hints and tips

OPEN-SHUTTER FLASH PHOTOGRAPHY

If you want to illuminate opposite sides of a large cave and have one flash just powerful enough to light up one side of the chamber at a time:

■ Mount your camera on the tripod and compose the picture you wish to take.

■ The helper holding the flash must have a clear path between the two points at which the flash must be fired. (Put a dim torch that cannot be viewed by the camera on the ground as guide.)

■ Get everyone with you to switch off their light.

■ With the camera set to 'B' mode, use a cable release to open the shutter.

■ Ask your helper to fire the flash at one wall. Let him move to the second position and fire the flash at the other wall. Only then close the shutter to take the picture. Your helper's silhouette will appear twice in the same photograph, but you have doubled the power of your flash gun.

■ Ensure that the camera cannot 'see' the charge light of the flash as your helper moves it, or you will have an unsightly line across your picture.

COMPOSITION AND MODELS

■ When composing the shot, use a bright light to ensure that your image is in focus. A bright torch shone directly onto the subject will do.

■ A modeling light mounted near the camera will highlight the dark boulders that always seem to creep into the foreground and ruin a great shot.

■ Cave photographs taken with the light source close to the lens tend to look flat. Move the light away to create deeper shadows and add depth.

■ Depth is also a problem if the camera has only a built-in flash and no external connector. You can use the built-in flash to trigger a remote one by attaching it to a slave flash trigger.

■ Ordinary flashes give off infrared light. Cover the built-in flash with a piece of exposed slide film to mask it. The infrared light will penetrate the film and trigger the remote slave, but prevent the built-in flash from exposing the foreground.

■ Use a slave flash that is sensitive to infrared.

■ Note that photography trips can be very boring for models and people who carry the equipment!

Caving locations & organizations

rather than going to search for a cave yourself, begin by looking for a reputable caving club. See the contacts list at the end of this chapter, surf the Internet, or enquire at your local outdoor outfitter or mountain club — they should be able to provide you with contact details.

The most important reason for joining a club is that caving is a potentially dangerous sport. Many clubs offer training and introductory courses for beginners, as well as organized outings. Joining a trip led by experienced cavers will reduce the dangers and risks significantly and enable you to learn from them. Another good incentive for joining a club is that many cavers are secretive about their favorite underground venues. In an effort to protect a fragile environment, the exact location is seldom broadcast for fear that the cave may be vandalized. You are much more likely to hear of worthwhile caves if you enquire through a club who will also be able to furnish you with the latest information regarding required gear, recent closures and exciting new discoveries.

When planning a caving trip to another country, it is considered polite to contact their national caving organization. If your local club cannot provide you with the relevant contact details, search on the Internet, or contact the embassy or government representative of the country you intend to visit. You may be required to pay for permits that will allow you to cave in a foreign country. Again, check with the embassy before setting off on your trip.

Caves of the world

A comprehensive coverage of caving regions worldwide would merit its own book and is not within the scope of this beginner's guide. This section presents a variety of limestone, as well as sandstone and volcanic caves. It does not provide details about the more exotic ice caves of Greenland or the salt caves of Israel.

Africa

In the past, Africa was not considered a particularly cave-rich continent because few people had taken the time to look for any. The discovery of several interesting locations by overseas expeditions and an emerging local caving scene has changed this view.

The major karst areas in northern Africa are situated in the mountainous regions of Morocco. The longest cave is currently Wit Tamdoun which has more than 18km (11 miles) of passages. The continent's deepest, Anou Ifflis, lies further east in Algeria and reaches a depth of 1170m (3800ft). The entire region holds much potential for further exciting discoveries.

Several caves were also discovered in the vast karst region of Ethiopia. The areas further west in Central Africa are not easily accessible and largely unexplored.

The limestone landscapes that are found along the eastern seaboard of East Africa in countries such as Kenya and Tanzania and the island of Zanzibar have a wealth of limestone caves that have already been extensively explored. This is a volcanic region which also offers lava tubes.

There has been much speleological activity in the southern part of Africa, with its abundance of exciting caves in many areas. The splendid karst regions of Namibia boast one of the world's largest underground lakes known as Dragon's Breath, which has a surface area of over 26,000m^2 (28,3000ft^2). Neighboring Zimbabwe has lime- and sandstone caves. The northern Chinhoyi region has several limestone caves worth exploring, while the Chimanimani mountain range offers several large and interesting sandstone caves and well-developed karst. Here you will find several caves that are over 100m (330ft) deep, with the

opposite DESCENDING INTO THE DEEP GOLONDRINAS PIT IN MEXICO IS A BREATHTAKING EXPERIENCE.

ONE OF SOUTHERN AFRICA'S MOST FASCINATING CAVE COMPLEXES, THE CANGO CAVES WERE DISCOVERED IN THE LATE 18TH CENTURY. EARLY EXPLORERS BRAVED THE DARKNESS OF THE VAST CAVERNS WITH HOMEMADE CANDLES.

Mawenge Mwena reaching as deep as 305m (1000ft). The southernmost tip of the African continent is taken up by South Africa, which has major karst regions in its Mpumalanga, Northern and Northern Cape provinces. Smaller areas also occur along the Southern Cape coast. In the Cape Province, both limestone and sandstone caves can be found, among them the world famous Cango Caves complex.

The island of Madagascar, lying some 412km (256 miles) east of mainland Africa, has become a very popular destination for international caving expeditions because it has large limestone areas along its western edge. Caves located in the island's northern parts, which are rather wet and tropical, have seen extensive exploration in the past, as have the drier southern regions that contain some of the deepest underground systems found on the island.

Asia

The large limestone region that covers much of central Asia has huge caving potential but is yet to be explored thoroughly. One system in Uzbekistan known as the Boj-Bulok has been surveyed to a depth of 1415m (4640ft).

China is well known for its magnificent tower karst and associated river caves. Although the caves are not particularly long they contain long passages and shafts. The Miao Room in the Gebihe Cave is one of the largest cave chambers in the world.

The Malaysian islands south of Asia contain numerous caves that are ideal for enthusiastic expedition cavers. Situated in the tropics, the islands enjoy a very high annual rainfall, and the abundance of water has turned the limestone regions into some of the most spectacular karst landscapes found anywhere on earth. Unfortunately, most of them lie deep inside the vast tropical rainforests, making access to the caves difficult. Furthermore, since the dense jungle canopy effectively blocks out the sun, the caves are continually damp — you need to take suitable gear with you.

Gunung Mulu National Park, a popular destination on the island of Borneo, is where you will find Deer Cave. Although only a kilometer or so in length it features a gigantic chamber with an average height of over 90m (295ft) throughout. The passage, believed to be the largest in the world, is never less than 70m (230ft) wide. The cave can only be visited as part of a tour.

The islands of Indonesia and Papua New Guinea are similar to Sarawak in that they, too, have large lime-stone regions virtually hidden beneath a lush tropical forest. Indonesia's longest cave system has over 50km (30 miles) of passages, while the deepest cave extends deeper than 1100m (3600ft) underground.

SO MASSIVE ARE THE DIMENSIONS OF BORNEO'S SARAWAK CHAMBER, THE LARGEST NATURAL ROCK CHAMBER IN THE WORLD, THAT IT CAN ACCOMMODATE 40 BOEING 747 AIRCRAFT WITH EASE.

A CAVER STOPS TO ADMIRE STALAGMITES AND STALCTITES IN OGOF FYNNON DDU, WALES.

caving potential existing in the Mendip Hills. Further exploration has revealed a host of other caves, including the tortuous Eastwater System (160m; 520ft deep) and the well decorated GB Cave (134m; 440ft deep).

Goatchurch Cavern and other short caves in the Burrington area make ideal caving venues for beginners and are frequently used to introduce eager novices to the sport.

The Forest of Dean boasts the Otter Hole near Chepstow with its many spectacular decorations, as well as the Slaughter Stream Cave which is 12km (7.5 miles) long. The large entrance to the show caves of Peak Cavern (15km; 9 miles) makes them the most famous in Derbyshire, but there are many lesser known cave systems that are also quite easy to explore.

Unlike the rest of the UK, Scotland is not known for large caves, although there are some very sporting flood-prone caves on the Isle of Skye. The limestone of Sutherland is the center of Scottish caving and provides underground locations that are suitable for both beginners and the more experienced caving community.

The limestone region of Southern Wales boasts Dan Yr Ogof (16km; 10

United Kingdom and Ireland

The United Kingdom is blessed with a large percentage of limestone and numerous caves. The limestone of Yorkshire, coupled with a very high rainfall, has led to a classic karst landscape. In this area you will find some famous systems such as Gaping Ghyll, Juniper Gulf and Alum Pot. To the west, in Cumbria and Lancashire, lies the massive Easegill System (70km; 43 miles long). Take heed of flood warnings when caving in this region.

The show caves at Cheddar and the ever popular Swildon's Hole (10km; 6 miles) give an indication of the

miles long) near Pen y Cae with its long straw formations and large passages. Nearby, the Ogof Fynnon Ddu system has a complicated maze on an upper level and active stream passages on lower levels. Further east, Ogof Draenen with a length of 66km (41 miles) is rapidly becoming the longest cave in the United Kingdom.

Mostly horizontal caves are found in Ireland's large limestone areas. The longest cave in this country is Poulnagollum (15km; 9 miles) in County Clare, while the deepest is Reyfod Pot (179m; 585ft deep), located in County Fermanagh.

Australia and New Zealand

One of the most important caving areas 'down under' is to be found in Tasmania, where dense forests cover much of the limestone, making exploration extremely difficult. Many of the caves in this region are very wet and make for some really sporting trips, provided you are adequately prepared.

The best-known caving area in Australia is found in the semi-arid Nullarbor Plain. Most of the caves here are horizontal and many are partially or completely flooded. The longest one in the region is Old Homestead Cave, now over 28km (17 miles) long.

Queensland Bluff, well known and much loved for its splendid tower karst, adds a different aspect to cave exploration: with internal cave temperatures continually hovering well above 30°C (86°F), wetsuits are unlikely to be a part of anyone's gear even though the caves are wet.

The isolated Kimberleys in the northwestern corner of Australia have tropical karst. Most of the known caves here are horizontal and getting to them can be a challenging expedition in itself.

New Zealand also has much to offer. Its deepest caves are to be found on the South Island in the regions of Mount Owen and Mount Arthur. Nettlebed Cave on Mount Arthur has a very complex system and is over 24km (15 miles) long and nearly 900m (2950ft) high. The North Island is better known for its horizontal cave systems. Of these, Waitomo Cave, with its mass of glow worms, is probably the most famous.

THE NORTHWEST OF NEW ZEALAND'S SOUTH ISLAND DISPLAYS MANY IMPRESSIVE KARST FORMATIONS, SUCH AS THE DRAMATIC OPARAPARA LIMESTONE ARCH IN THE KAHURANGI NATIONAL PARK, WHICH IS A FIRM FAVORITE WITH CAVERS.

POSTOJNSKA JAMA IS SLOVENIA'S LONGEST CAVE SYSTEM AND ONE OF THE FEW PLACES WHERE THE *PROTEUS ANGUINUS* SALAMANDER, ENDEMIC TO THE COUNTRY AND THE LARGEST CAVE-DWELLING VERTEBRATE KNOWN, CAN BE SPOTTED.

Europe

Europe, the birthplace of caving, offers many easily accessible karst regions and some of the world's longest and deepest known caves.

France and Spain share the many sinkholes and river caves occuring in the Pyrenees mountain range that straddles both countries. Some of the rivers here plunge into caves on one side of an international border and re-emerge in a different country. Although the region has been extensively explored for over 100 years, there is still much to be done. Two of the world's five deepest caves are located in France, among them Réseau Jean (1602m; 5250ft) and Gouffre Mirolda (1616m; 5300ft), both in the Haute-Savoie area. Spain also has its fair share of deep caves, including Torca del Cerro (1589m; 5210ft) and Sistema del Trave (1441m; 4755ft).

In Italy, caving has also long been a popular outdoor pursuit due to the vast number that exist there. Deep and wet cave systems can be found at both the eastern and western ends of the Italian Alps.

At an impressive 1249m (4100ft), the Abisso Paolo Roversi is the deepest Italian cave, with Abisso Ulivifer at 1215m (3990ft) not far behind. Further to the south in the Apennines, there are large areas of karst still waiting to be explored.

Switzerland too has many caves and a very strong caving tradition. The picturesque Oberland region in central Switzerland is a major caving area with much potential for deep cave systems that have hitherto remained undiscovered. The Siebenhengste-Hohgant system is 145km (90 miles) long and 1340m (4390ft) deep. Alpine neighbor Austria, too, has a very long caving history. It, too, is well known for its many deep systems. Austrian caves are especially famous for their wonderful ice formations that remain frozen all year round. Of the countless systems surveyed in this country, at least 11 are deeper than 1000m (3280ft), the deepest being Lamprechtshofen at 1632m (5350ft).

(This cave is currently also the world's second deepest cave; much of the original exploration was done from the bottom up.)

The term karst was first used in Slovenia to describe the landscape created by a dissolving layer of rock. And indeed, this Eastern European country boasts some very impressive karst features. They include Ceki, at 1480m (4850ft) the deepest cave in Slovenia, and Postonjska Jama, which is the longest cave in this country and stretches for 19km (11.8 miles).

The Ukraine is one of the most important areas of gypsum karst in the world. This type of karst typically results in cave formations that have a maze-like network of passages. Optimisticeskaja, the second longest cave in the world, occurs here. It has an incredible 212km (131 miles) of surveyed passages.

The Caucasus between the Black and Caspian seas in southwestern Russia and the limestone of Georgia near the Caspian Sea are both relatively new caving areas with huge potential. Veronja Cave in Abkhazia, Georgia, recently took the title of the world's deepest cave with a depth of 1710m (5610ft).

USA

The vast North American continent is blessed with splendid areas of limestone and numerous caves, and a growing number of cavers come to explore these hidden wonders. In the northeast of the country there are many small caves in the Appalachian fold belt, while the Appalachian Plateau further west also has large areas of limestone. Since part of this extremely cave-rich area covers the states of Tennessee, Alabama and Georgia, it is known among cavers as the TAG region. This area features many deep multi-level caves. One of the most famous of these is Ellison Cave (1063m; 3490ft), which has spectacular vertical shafts.

Kentucky is home to the Mammoth Cave, which has a staggering surveyed length in excess of 570km (354 miles). Widely regarded as the most famous cave in the world, exploration of Mammoth continues unabated and new cave passages with gypsum crystal formations are discovered each year.

Limestone on the Ozark Plateau covers the greater part of Missouri, where caves are mostly horizontal and few are longer than 20km (12 miles) in length.

above THE ENTRANCE TO KENTUCKY'S MAMMOTH CAVE, WHICH HAS BEEN EXTENSIVELY EXPLORED AND IS ONE OF THE BEST KNOWN CAVE SYSTEMS IN THE WORLD.

right A MASSIVE STALAGMITE UNDER A CURTAIN OF STALACTITES IN THE CARLSBAD CAVERNS NATIONAL PARK, WHICH HOUSES MANY AMAZING CAVE DECORATIONS.

HUGE, ICE-WHITE CRYSTALS FORM THE BREATHTAKING CHANDELIER IN THE FAMOUS CHANDELIER BALLROOM IN LECHUGILLA, NEW MEXICO, ONE OF THE MOST SPECTACULARLY DECORATED CAVES IN THE WORLD.

Caves in the highlands of central Texas form part of interesting fossil systems that have extensive calcite decorations. Apart from the many small caves in South Dakota, two very long and complex maze-cave systems can be found in the southern United States: Wind Cave at 56km (35 miles), and Jewel Cave which is currently the seventh longest in the world with around 200km (125 miles) of passages.

Carlsbad Caverns National Park in the Guadalupe Mountains of New Mexico is home to two unique cave systems known as Carlsbad Caverns and Lechugilla Cave. Rising groundwater rich in sulphuric acid sculpted these caves from the surrounding limestone. This has resulted in deep, long cave systems with large passages and chambers, as well as some very unusual cave decorations. The justifiably famous Chandelier Ballroom has gypsum crystals that are over 3m (10ft) long.

Irrespective of its abundance of caving regions, the deepest American cave does not occur on the mainland. Kazumura Cave, a lava tube on the Island of Hawaii holds this honor. It is over 60km (37 miles) long and 1100m (3610ft) deep.

Central America

Towering mountains, plentiful limestone and a high annual rainfall are the factors that have made eastern Mexico such a premier caving destination. The Yucatán Peninsula is a large low-lying limestone plateau that is characterized by deep water-filled sinkholes. Further south lies the thick mass of the Huautla Plateau, which is permeated with deep caves.

The limestone development continues further south into Guatemala and Belize. Much of Guatemala is covered in well-developed karst and there are literally hundreds of known caves here. The Chiquibul River region has many caves with large passages.

South America

The largest limestone area in South America occurs in Brazil where there are countless small caves to explore. Most of them are rather shallow with few reaching 100m (330ft). There are also limestone and volcanic caves further south in Chile.

Although Venezuela also has a number of limestone caves, it is far better known for its outstanding sandstone karst. The large sandstone table mountains known locally as *tepui* enjoy a very high tropical rainfall. This has led to the formation of some of the deepest sandstone caves in the world, with the Aonda System reaching 382m (1250ft).

BELIZE CHAMBER IN BELIZE, CENTRAL AMERICA, IS ONE OF THE LARGEST KNOWN NATURAL CAVE CHAMBERS IN THE WORLD.

Caving Organizations

Although there is no global controlling body, the International Union of Speleology (Union Internationale de Spéléologie, UIS) has over 50 member countries that disseminate caving information.

Australia
- AUSTRALIAN SPELEOLOGICAL FEDERATION INC.
- P.O. Box 388
- Broadway
- New South Wales, 2007
- Website: www.caves.org.au/

Belgium
- THE YELLOW PAGES OF CAVING IN BELGIUM
- Website: users.skynet.be/sky75112

- VERBOND VAN VLAAMSE SPELEOLOGEN
- Broekstraat 23
- B-3001 Heverlee
- Tel: (16) 23 78 99
- Fax: (16) 22 74 96
- E-mail: vvs@speleo.be
- Website: www.speleo.be.vvs/index.htm

Brazil
- SOCIEDADE BRASILEIRA DE ESPELEOLOGIA
- Caixa Postal 234
- 70.359-970
- Brasília
- Website: www.sbe.com.br

Canada
- ALBERTA SPELEOLOGICAL SOCIETY
- Website: www.caving.ab.ca
- BRITISH COLUMBIA SPELEOLOGICAL FEDERATION
- P.O. Box 8124
- Station Central Post Office
- Victoria, BC
- V8W 3R8
- E-mail: bcsf@cancaver.ca
- Website: www.cancaver.ca/

- SOCIÉTÉ QUÉBÉCOISE DE SPÉLÉOLOGIE
- 4545, av. Pierre-de-Coubertin
- C.P. 1000, Succ. M
- Montréal (Québec), H1V 3R2
- Tel: (514) 252 3006
- Fax: (514) 252 3201
- E-mail: info-sqs@speleo.qc.ca
- Website: www.speleo.qc.ca

- TORONTO CAVING GROUP
- 78 King High Avenue
- Downsview
- Ontario, M3H 3B1
- E-mail (c/o Kirk MacGregor): kirkm@globalserve.net
- Website: www.trigger.net/~tcg/

France
- LA FÉDÉRATION FRANÇAISE DE SPÉLÉOLOGIE
- Tel: (1) 43 57 56 54
- Fax: (1) 49 23 00 95
- E-mail: FFS.paris@wanadoo.fr
- Website: www.ffspeleo.fr

Germany
- GERMAN SPELEOLOGICAL FEDERATION (VDHK)
- Hehner Strasse 100
- 41069 Mönchengladbach
- E-mail: Michael.Laumanns@bmf.bund.de
- Website: www.vdhk.de/

- VEREIN FÜR HÖHLENKUNDE IN MÜNCHEN E.V.
- Postfach 202030
- D-80020
- München
- E-mail: adolf.triller@t-online.de
- Website: www.vhm-muenchen.de/

Caving Organizations

Ireland
- SPELEOLOGICAL UNION OF IRELAND
- c/o Association for Adventure Sports (A.F.A.S.)
- House of Sport
- Long Mile Road
- Walkinstown
- Dublin 12
- E-mail: suisecretary@cavingireland.org
- Website: www.cavingireland.org/

New Zealand
- NEW ZEALAND SPELEOLOGICAL SOCIETY
- P.O. Box 18
- Waitomo Caves
- Website: www.massey.ac.nz/~sglasgow/nzss/

South Africa
- SOUTH AFRICAN SPELEOLOGICAL ASSOCIATION
- P.O. Box 4812
- Cape Town, 8000
- Website: sasa.caving.org.za

Switzerland
- SPELEOLOGICAL SOCIETY OF SWITZERLAND
- Case postale 1332
- CH-2301 La Chaux-de-Fonds
- Tel: (0) 32 913 3533
- Fax: (0) 32 913 3555
- E-mail: SSS-SGH@speleo.ch
- Website: www.speleo.ch/

United Kingdom
- NATIONAL CAVING ASSOCIATION (The National Body for Caving in England, Scotland and Wales)
- c/o Monomark House
- 27 Old Gloucester St
- London, WC1N 3XX
- E-mail: admin@nca.org.uk
- Website: www.nca.org.uk

- BRITISH CAVE RESEARCH ASSOCIATION
- The Old Methodist Chapel
- Great Hucklow
- Buxton, Derbyshire, SK17 8RG
- Tel: (1785) 25 8979
- Website: www.bcra.org.uk

- THE GRAMPIAN SPELEOLOGICAL GROUP
- 8 Scone Gardens
- Edinburgh, EH8 7DQ
- Scotland
- E-mail: gsg-info@sat.dundee.ac.uk
- Website: www.sat.dundee.ac.uk/~arb/gsg/

USA
- THE NATIONAL SPELEOLOGICAL SOCIETY
- 2813 Cave Avenue
- Huntsville, AL 35810-4413 (Alabama)
- Tel: (256) 852 1300
- Website: www.caves.org/

- NATIONAL CAVES ASSOCIATION
(Show caves in USA)
- P.O. Box 206
- Park City, KY 42160 (Kentucky)
- Website: www.cavern.com

Useful websites

- **International Union of Speleology (UIS)**
rubens.its.unimelb.edu.au/~pgm/uis/index.html
- **Guide to Single Rope Techniques (SRT)**
www.cavepage.magna.com.au/cave/SRT.html
- **Russian website with many caving club links**
fadr.msu.ru/~sigalov/
- **Long and deep caves of the world (Bob Gulden)**
www.pipeline.com/~caverbob/home.html
This website was the main source for checking lengths and depths of caves mentioned in the locations section.

Glossary

abseil Descending a steep slope or pitch with the help of a harness and descending devices attached to a rope.

active caves Caves that contain large quantities of flowing water and are still actively forming.

anchor A cave wall or solid rock to which a rope is firmly and securely attached when rigging a pitch.

aragonite Crystal form of calcium carbonate often found in caves; looks like whiskers or hair-like spikes.

ascender Self-locking device that is slid up a tensioned rope, allowing the climber to ascend.

battery A number of cells connected in series (positive to negative) to produce a higher voltage.

belay This can have two meanings:
a) Caver One protects Caver Two from falling, by controlling a rope securely attached to Caver Two;
b) a rope firmly anchored to a rock.

belayer Person protecting another climber.

bobbin A simple type of descender.

bolt Metal expansion device fastened into a predrilled hole in a rockface; used as artificial anchor for belays.

calcite Colorless or white mineral form of calcium carbonate that causes cave decorations like flowstones, stalagmites and stalactites.

carabiner A metal link with a spring-loaded opening (gate) that is used to attach slings and ropes for protection when climbing.

carbide A calcium carbide compound that reacts with water to produce acetylene, a colorless but slightly smelly flammable gas that produces a bright light.

carbide lamp Caving light that contains carbide and burns with a naked flame (still widely used for caving).

carbonate rocks Family of mineral rocks comprising: hard blue limestone, calcite decorations and dolomite.

cave pearl Calcite decoration formed like a sphere.

cell A single unit with a particular chemistry that is able to produce electrical energy.

cenote A water-filled sinkhole formed by a collapsing top layer of limestone crust.

clinometer An instrument for measuring the angle of inclination between two points, relative to the horizon.

compass An instrument that determines direction by measuring the bearing between points relative to the earth's magnetic field.

conglomerate Rock made up of pebbles or smaller stone fragments, cemented together by compact sand.

descender Friction device used for abseiling.

deviation Junction at which a rope is redirected away from a cave wall with the help of a carabiner or cord.

doline Shallow type of funnel-shaped sinkhole caused by solution in limestone regions.

duck Short portion of a cave passage that is almost completely filled with water.

dynamic rope Rope that has an elastic core surrounded by a tightly woven protective outer layer, designed to absorb the shock of a fall by stretching (commonly used in rock climbing).

flagging tape Plastic tape used to mark a path through a cave or protect sensitive sections.

flowstone Calcite deposit (sometimes of considerable thickness) that covers a rockface.

formations Collective term for calcite cave decorations (stalagmites, stalactites, flowstone and helictites, etc.).

fossil passage Older upper levels of a cave system that were left high and dry when the water table dropped.

friction device Artificial device that increases the resistance between two objects (such as a descending caver's body and a rope) to lower the rate of speed.

frog rig Simple climbing system used in SRT.

gypsum Hydrated calcium sulphate that can form delicate flower-like cave decorations.

hanger A metal ring or plate screwed into an expansion device for use as an anchor on vertical pitches.

harness Essential caving gear consisting of waist belt and loops for the legs, designed to comfortably support a caver's full body weight on pitches.

helictites Cave decorations formed when crystallization is faster than gravity, leading to spectacularly twisted forms that grow in all directions.

hypothermia Potentially fatal condition caused when the body's core temperature sinks too low.

karst Limestone area displaying typical features such as sinkholes, indicating good caving areas.

lava Hot, molten rock (magma) emanating from the earth or a volcano.

lava tube The outer 'shell' of an old lava flow (a cave formed when the outer layer of a flow cooled, providing a sheath in which hot lava continued to flow).

LED Light-emitting diodes, a solid-state lightbulb.

lumen Unit used to measure light output.

maillon rapide Metal link used as a connector, featuring a threaded cylinder rather than a hinged snap-gate.

mantle Layer of the earth between crust and core.

memory effect This results when a partially discharged NiCad (nickel-cadmium) battery is recharged — it will only remember the top-up part of the charge.

phreatic passage A phreas is a permanently flooded section of the earth. Cave passages formed in this zone (phreatic passages) typically have a symmetrical round or oval cross section.

pitch The vertical section of a climb.

pseudokarst A non-limestone region that looks like one, displaying many limestone features and especially caves.

rack A type of descender.

rappel *see* abseil.

re-belay The point at which an SRT rope is reattached to a cave wall, partway down a pitch.

resurgence This is where cave water emerges onto the surface (also known as rising or spring).

rig A technique used to ascend, descend or traverse using a network of safety ropes and anchors to transport cavers and their equipment.

rope walking A fast SRT technique used for climbing up a single rope.

sea cave Cave formed along a coastline by wave action, where the sea erodes weak points in the shoreline.

shale Compressed layers of clay sediment forming a darkish and very finely grained laminated rock.

sinkhole Depression in the ground, often water-filled, formed by the collapse of an underground limestone chamber. These are often entrances to extensive caves. (Also known as a doline.)

slave flash The device enabling remote triggering of the flashlight (useful for cave photography).

soda straw A long and thin, hollow stalactite.

speleology The scientific study of caves to determine their geological age, formation, fauna and flora.

SRT Single Rope Technique, a method for descending and ascending vertical pitches using only one rope to explore an underground cave.

stalactite A cave decoration made of calcium carbonate that hangs from the ceiling of a limestone cave.

stalagmite Cave decoration made of calcium carbonate that grows from the floor of a limestone cave, often caused by water dripping from a stalactite above it.

static rope Rope that has little elasticity (as opposed to a dynamic rope) and is generally used for caving, especially in SRT techniques.

stop A type of descender.

stratum Any distinct layer of sedimentary rock. (Plural: strata.)

sump Cave passage that is completely filled with water.

talus cave A cave formed between the huge boulders found at the foot of a mountain. (Also known as scree.)

tectonic Forces within the earth's crust that deform and distort the upper layers of the earth.

theodolite An instrument used by surveyors to measure horizontal and vertical angles.

topography The surface features (such as mountains, valleys and sinkholes) that define the character of a particular region.

topographical map A survey map showing the surface features of a region (with height indications).

travertine A porous rock made of calcium carbonate and deposited by ground or surface water.

vadose passage Passage formed by swift-flowing water.

vertical crack A deep crack formed when tectonic forces distorted and ripped apart the earth's crust, which was subsequently tilted at a steep angle.

washout cave Caves formed when soil or gravel is washed out by flowing water.

Watt (W) Unit of power used to indicate the strength of light bulbs.

Index

Photographic credits